# CONTENTS

# COMMEMORATIVE COIN LEGISLATION AND RELATED ISSUES IN THE 103RD CONGRESS

## HEARING

BEFORE THE

SUBCOMMITTEE ON CONSUMER CREDIT AND INSURANCE

OF THE

COMMITTEE ON BANKING, FINANCE AND URBAN AFFAIRS

HOUSE OF REPRESENTATIVES

ONE HUNDRED THIRD CONGRESS

FIRST SESSION

NOVEMBER 10, 1993

Printed for the use of the Committee on Banking, Finance and Urban Affairs

**Serial No. 103–98**

U.S. GOVERNMENT PRINTING OFFICE

73–932 CC WASHINGTON : 1994

For sale by the U.S. Government Printing Office
Superintendent of Documents, Congressional Sales Office, Washington, DC 20402
ISBN 0-16-046162-6

## HOUSE COMMITTEE ON BANKING, FINANCE AND URBAN AFFAIRS

HENRY B. GONZALEZ, Texas, *Chairman*

STEPHEN L. NEAL, North Carolina
JOHN J. LAFALCE, New York
BRUCE F. VENTO, Minnesota
CHARLES E. SCHUMER, New York
BARNEY FRANK, Massachusetts
PAUL E. KANJORSKI, Pennsylvania
JOSEPH P. KENNEDY II, Massachusetts
FLOYD H. FLAKE, New York
KWEISI MFUME, Maryland
MAXINE WATERS, California
LARRY LAROCCO, Idaho
BILL ORTON, Utah
JIM BACCHUS, Florida
HERBERT C. KLEIN, New Jersey
CAROLYN B. MALONEY, New York
PETER DEUTSCH, Florida
LUIS V. GUTIERREZ, Illinois
BOBBY L. RUSH, Illinois
LUCILLE ROYBAL-ALLARD, California
THOMAS M. BARRETT, Wisconsin
ELIZABETH FURSE, Oregon
NYDIA M. VELAZQUEZ, New York
ALBERT R. WYNN, Maryland
CLEO FIELDS, Louisiana
MELVIN WATT, North Carolina
MAURICE HINCHEY, New York
CALVIN M. DOOLEY, California
RON KLINK, Pennsylvania
ERIC FINGERHUT, Ohio

JAMES A. LEACH, Iowa
BILL McCOLLUM, Florida
MARGE ROUKEMA, New Jersey
DOUG BEREUTER, Nebraska
THOMAS J. RIDGE, Pennsylvania
TOBY ROTH, Wisconsin
ALFRED A. (AL) McCANDLESS, California
RICHARD H. BAKER, Louisiana
JIM NUSSLE, Iowa
CRAIG THOMAS, Wyoming
SAM JOHNSON, Texas
DEBORAH PRYCE, Ohio
JOHN LINDER, Georgia
JOE KNOLLENBERG, Michigan
RICK LAZIO, New York
ROD GRAMS, Minnesota
SPENCER BACHUS, Alabama
MIKE HUFFINGTON, California
MICHAEL CASTLE, Delaware
PETER KING, New York

BERNARD SANDERS, Vermont

---

### SUBCOMMITTEE ON CONSUMER CREDIT AND INSURANCE

JOSEPH P. KENNEDY II, Massachusetts, *Chairman*

HENRY B. GONZALEZ, Texas
LARRY LAROCCO, Idaho
LUIS V. GUTIERREZ, Illinois
BOBBY L. RUSH, Illinois
LUCILLE ROYBAL-ALLARD, California
THOMAS M. BARRETT, Wisconsin
ELIZABETH FURSE, Oregon
NYDIA M. VELAZQUEZ, New York
ALBERT R. WYNN, Maryland
CLEO FIELDS, Louisiana
MELVIN WATT, North Carolina
MAURICE HINCHEY, New York
PAUL E. KANJORSKI, Pennsylvania
FLOYD H. FLAKE, New York
MAXINE WATERS, California
CAROLYN B. MALONEY, New York
PETER DEUTSCH, Florida

ALFRED A. (AL) McCANDLESS, California
MICHAEL CASTLE, Delaware
PETER KING, New York
DEBORAH PRYCE, Ohio
JOHN LINDER, Georgia
JOE KNOLLENBERG, Michigan
DOUG BEREUTER, Nebraska
CRAIG THOMAS, Wyoming
RICK LAZIO, New York
ROD GRAMS, Minnesota
SPENCER BACHUS, Alabama
RICHARD H. BAKER, Louisiana

BERNARD SANDERS, Vermont

# COMMEMORATIVE COIN LEGISLATION AND RELATED ISSUES IN THE 103RD CONGRESS

---

**WEDNESDAY, NOVEMBER 10, 1993**

HOUSE OF REPRESENTATIVES,
SUBCOMMITTEE ON CONSUMER CREDIT AND INSURANCE,
COMMITTEE ON BANKING, FINANCE AND URBAN AFFAIRS,
*Washington, DC.*

The subcommittee met, pursuant to notice, at 2:45 p.m., in room 2220, Rayburn House Office Building, Hon. Joseph P. Kennedy [chairman of the subcommittee] presiding.

Present: Chairman Kennedy, Representatives Fields, Waters, McCandless, and Linder.

Chairman KENNEDY. Good to see you all here today. The subcommittee will please come to order.

This afternoon, the subcommittee considers four proposals to establish commemorative coin programs. They are: H.R. 535, the Prisoner of War Coin Act; H.R. 789, the Jefferson Coin Act; H.R. 1608, the Vietnam Veterans Memorial Coin Act; and H.R. 1697, the Women in Military Service Coin Act. Each of these bills has over 218 cosponsors, as required by the rules of the subcommittee to hold a hearing. I might add that, as of today, these are the only coin bills in the House that have the requisite number of cosponsors.

Each of these bills also furthers a very worthy cause. I look forward to hearing from their distinguished authors shortly.

The Constitution grants to Congress the power of coinage. The rules of the House and of the committee invest that power in this subcommittee. During my brief tenure as chairman of this subcommittee, I have learned more about the coinage than I ever thought possible. Maybe I would have changed the wording of that sentence a little bit, but nevertheless, several truths have become apparent.

First, there has been a proliferation of coin proposals in the Congress in recent years. Many of them, including the ones before us today, have great merit; others do not.

Second, coin programs can raise a great deal of money for the causes they are earmarked to fund. Often they raise more money than can be found by the normal appropriations process.

Third, the organizations upon which the government confers the right to receive the proceeds of coin sales are subject to little, if any, government oversight. The *Washington Times* recently reported that the Battle of Normandy Foundation, which has received $3 million from a coin to build a memorial at Normandy has spent 90 percent of its money on travel, entertainment, fund-raising, and the personal expenses of its President, a man named Tony Stout. To my knowledge, the memorial is yet to be built and may never be built.

Fourth, and finally, the proliferation of coins in the market is having a negative impact on the sales of each coin. Although each coin program may have its own unique constituency, the Mint tells us that, by and large, the bulk of the market consists of 2 million or so devoted coin collectors. In fact, the Mint tells us that 90 percent of the coins sold in a typical program go to the same collectors.

Over the last 7 years, there have been 12 commemorative coins put onto the market. On average, these coins are selling less and less, because supply is outpacing the demand.

It is clear to me that we need to reform the way we go about enacting and overseeing the commemorative coin programs. We don't want to kill the goose that lays the golden eggs by saturating the market and driving prices so low that no organization can meet its goals.

Accordingly, it is my intention to pursue, with Mr. McCandless and others members of the subcommittee and the Mint, several changes in the minting process. I would suggest that we consider the following steps:

One, a cap on the number of coins that can be enacted in any one year to be determined on the advice of the Coin Commission established in the last Congress.

Two, GAO audits of foundations that receive and spend the proceeds of coin sales, along with quarterly financial reporting to the Mint in order to prevent waste and abuse.

Third, requiring these foundations to share in some of the upfront costs of minting in order to prove their seriousness.

Fourth, ensuring that any windfalls in the sale of coins be shared by the Treasury and not hoarded by a given coin foundation. Let's not forget, it is only because of the government's unique power to mint that foundations can raise millions of dollars. I don't think it is too much that we ask that the taxpayers that support the government share some of the benefits.

I want to thank all of the witnesses for appearing this afternoon and, in particular, Congressmen Bonior, Ridge, Peterson, and L.F. Payne. I also want to thank Mr. Essner from the Mint and our other witnesses for taking the time to fit into Congress' busy schedule the important testimony that they will provide.

We also appreciate all of your cooperation and all of your interest in seeing these coins come to pass. I know that many of the people in our audience today have very important causes which they believe very strongly in. We want to see the four coins that have been proposed. All have tremendous merit for their particular mission and purposes for which you have worked so diligently to get the proper number of signatures. We appreciate the hard work that many of you have put into the specific effort.

[The prepared statement of Mr. Kennedy can be found in the appendix.]

We appreciate the Members of Congress being willing to come forward, and we look forward to their testimony this afternoon.

Mr. Peterson. Mr. Peterson, please proceed.

## STATEMENT OF HON. DOUGLAS "PETE" PETERSON, A REPRESENTATIVE IN CONGRESS FROM THE STATE OF FLORIDA

Mr. PETERSON. Thank you, Mr. Chairman. I appreciate the opportunity to testify before you. I will be brief.

You have covered, of course, the merits of the Coin bill that I have before you, the POW Coin bill. The purpose of the coin that we want to have minted is, first and foremost, to honor the many POWs. There are over 142,000 POWs that are on record through this Nation's history who served with valor, and in many cases, have given their lives for their Nation in the process of their capture.

We have, though, also an opportunity here to use this as a vehicle for funding the only museum that has been set aside at Andersonville Prison in Andersonville, Georgia, to place the artifacts and the history of the POWs that have served this great land. It is an oversight—I think not purposeful. It just is simply that we haven't done it. It is kind of an ugly part of our personal history in that we have had to relive those events in our lives, that—those of us who served in those capacities; yet we also understand that it is very important to the history of this country to have the public reminded from time to time, through visitation and through the museum, that these things happen, and that it is part of war, and that there is survival as a result of those kinds of things, and that there is courage and sacrifice necessary as part of service.

So what we are trying to do is fund the final segments of the events in Andersonville.

I would note that we have already put some appropriated money in; there has been private fund-raising to date that will continue, and what this is going to do—we hope that the first $3 million of the receipts of the coin sales would help complete the museum, would put another $1 million into an endowment to make sure that that place stays in good order and is maintained properly and that the exhibits are updated as necessary.

And then whatever would be remaining after having sold 1,500,000 of these coins, then that would go toward the maintenance of the national cemeteries which have been so poorly funded over the past several years.

We have limited the number of coins that we want to mint, and that is on purpose so that we can't and don't get the collectors to a point where we are maxing out the public. But I am absolutely confident that as of right now, there are over 66,000 former POWs still alive, and with their extended families and with the veterans' groups and with all of the constituencies that I would foresee to purchase this coin, we have certainly enough interest to sell that many coins, and that is all.

We would then end the mintage and that would be not only a collector's item, but something that we could have as a museum for the placement of these artifacts of which we speak.

I will stop there. I won't take any questions, but I would ask that my statement be made a part of the record and I appreciate the opportunity to testify today.

[The prepared statement of Mr. Peterson can be found in the appendix.]

Chairman KENNEDY. I want to indicate just how avidly you have lobbied for this coin. I know that this is an issue that obviously means a great deal to you personally, but also the commitment that you have made to other POWs really shows the intent of Congress. I think anyone who follows this issue and knows of your burning commitment to soldiers that have fought the good fight and suffered so tremendously for our country ought to recognize the extent of your dedication.

I very much want to say how impressed I am by the commitment that you have shown, and am glad that we are going to be able to move forward. I also appreciate the consideration that you have— and the other Members that are testifying have provided me as the chairman of this Subcommittee in dealing with all of the numismatic issues that have arisen.

Thank you very much.

Mr. PETERSON. Well, we appreciate your comments and also your patience, as I have been leaning pretty hard on you personally over these last several months.

Chairman KENNEDY. I think my arm is going to straighten out in a couple of months here, Pete.

Mr. PETERSON. But I appreciate that very much.

Chairman KENNEDY. Then I have to get the pain off my other arm. Well, we will do everything we can to make this happen.

Mr. PETERSON. Thank you.

Chairman KENNEDY. Mr. Ridge.

Mr. RIDGE. Mr. Chairman, I would be pleased to defer to my colleague on his coin, awaiting the arrival of our colleague, Congressman Bonior, so I could testify with Jan Scruggs as well.

[The prepared statement of Mr. Bonior can be found in the appendix.]

Chairman KENNEDY. Certainly. We look forward to your testimony.

And now the fellow who has been squeezing my left arm for the last several months, who has shown more innovative and creative ways to get us to move on this bill than any single Member of Congress, L.F. Payne. L.F., it is good to have you here, and we are looking forward to your testimony.

## STATEMENT OF HON. L.F. PAYNE, A REPRESENTATIVE IN CONGRESS FROM THE STATE OF VIRGINIA

Mr. PAYNE. Thank you, Mr. Chairman, and thank you for holding this hearing today. We all very much appreciate that.

And I thank my colleague, Mr. Ridge, for allowing me to go first.

Thank you for taking up this bill, H.R. 789, which is a coin commemorating the 250th anniversary of Thomas Jefferson's birth. I want to thank all who are cosponsors of this bill. This is a bipartisan bill, it is supported by all of the Members of our Virginia delegation, it currently has 253 cosponsors in the House and is one of only two Coin bills that have already passed the Senate.

I am doing this because Monticello, the home of Thomas Jefferson, and Poplar Forest, his second home, both are in my congressional district.

This is an important year for Thomas Jefferson. President Clinton began his inaugural celebration at Monticello, in honor of

Thomas Jefferson, who is the architect of our democratic government. The spirit of celebration has extended long past our borders. When Vaclav Havel was here, he talked about what Jefferson meant to Czechs as they started their own democratic system there in recent years.

Also, former Soviet President Gorbachev was at Monticello on Thomas Jefferson's birthday and made some remarks about how much Thomas Jefferson had meant to him and to many of the events that have occurred as the cold war was ended. It is because of these kinds of things that I had introduced H.R. 789 and why I have argued for its passage this year.

I believe that this coin will reach a constituency that extends well beyond the usual community of coin collectors. Monticello alone expects to have close to a quarter of a million visitors during the rest of this year, and I think that many of these visitors would appreciate the opportunity to further honor Thomas Jefferson by purchasing a coin in his honor.

This bill was drafted with careful consideration for the concerns that this subcommittee has expressed about the Coin bills and authorizes a very small number of coins to be issued, about 600,000; and the $1 denomination was selected to make the coin more affordable to the general public. The only other coin authorized under such limitations, which is the White House Coin bill, sold out in its entire issue in about 10 days; and we believe that this coin will likely do as well.

There are a number of projects that will be supported by this coin that relate to Monticello. In the case of Monticello, the proceeds from H.R. 789 will fund Monticello's first general endowment, and it will advance its primary mission of education and preservation.

Dan Jordan is here who heads up Monticello and who is the executive director of the foundation. He will speak specifically about the uses of the coin proceeds at Monticello.

I would also mention that Poplar Forest, which was Thomas Jefferson's personal retreat, which he designed and which he constructed, would also be a beneficiary of a portion of the proceeds of the coin; and the foundation attempting to save Poplar Forest for future generations faces a very daunting task. I have here some photographs of Poplar Forest that I would like to give to the subcommittee and to put into the record.

I would also ask that a statement from the officials at Poplar Forest be put into the record concerning their uses of the coin proceeds.

Chairman KENNEDY. Without objection, it is so ordered.

[The photographs and statement referred to can be found in the appendix.]

Mr. PAYNE. Mr. Chairman, when this Nation commemorated the 200th anniversary of Jefferson's birth, Congress passed legislation authorizing the construction of the Jefferson Memorial on The Mall. I believe that authorizing the minting of a commemorative coin in his honor is the least that we can do now as we celebrate the 250th anniversary of his birth.

I understand that later today we may hear some testimony that would suggest that this coin might be referred to some commission that is not yet established. I would say that Thomas Jefferson's 250th birth year is this year, 1993, and I would urge the subcommittee and the committee to act on this expeditiously, so that we might have this coin sold at a relevant time.

Thank you very much.

[The prepared statement of Mr. Payne can be found in the appendix.]

Chairman KENNEDY. Thank you very much for your excellent testimony, Mr. Payne. I have had a meeting with the Mint about the time sensitivity of your particular issue, because of the 250th anniversary passing this year, and we are looking to try and find a way to expedite the particular coin that you are interested in seeing minted. We are trying to come up with a way to make that happen. I have spoken directly with representatives of the Mint, including Gene Essner, the Deputy Director who is largely responsible for the place these days, to find a way to expedite the process.

If you have a few minutes at some point, L.F., I would suggest that you spend some time with him to just kind of get up to speed on some of their concerns and ways that these issues might be worked out.

Now, does that complete your testimony?

Mr. PAYNE. That completes my testimony. Thank you very much.

Chairman KENNEDY. We appreciate your participation very much. I think every American recognizes the contribution that Thomas Jefferson made to our country. There can be no individual in our Nation's history whose life is more deserving of this kind of commemoration, and also the kind of support that a memorial to President Jefferson so desperately needs.

We are looking forward to getting you the support that you need.

Mr. PAYNE. Thank you.

Chairman KENNEDY. Thank you very much.

Mr. Ridge, as a member of our Veterans' Committee, is well aware, as is Ms. Waters—that there have been several major problems in getting the Department of Defense to recognize the potential of biological, chemical, and nerve warfare that might have been present in our Persian Gulf conflict. We have been working very, very hard to deal with the concerns of many of our Nation's veterans that have been largely, to be honest with you, ignored by the Department of Defense.

We have had a couple of classified briefings canceled in the last couple of weeks. Finally, this morning, the Department of Defense sent an Assistant Secretary up to brief Members of Congress. Even that briefing only lasted for about 1½ hours. We asked the Assistant Secretary to come back to address Members that have a keen interest in this issue and the only time that he could find to come back is at 3 o'clock, which is right now. So I hope that the veterans in the audience will understand if I excuse myself for a few minutes to go downstairs to attend this briefing.

I think it is very, very important to our Nation's veterans, whose testimony would bring tears to your eyes in terms of what they have had to go through. I mean, Tom and I sat through a very long hearing yesterday and heard just unbelievable testimony about what our veterans have had to withstand and the denials that have taken place by our government.

So if you don't mind, I would like to excuse myself for a few minutes to go downstairs.

Ms. Waters, you look like a chairperson to me. I ask Maxine to take over, but please don't take it as any lack of interest on my part for this issue.

Tom, if you don't mind testifying.

Mr. RIDGE. Please. Thank you.

Chairman KENNEDY. Thank you.

Ms. WATERS [presiding]. Thank you very much.

Congressman, would you proceed with your testimony.

## STATEMENT OF HON. TOM RIDGE, A REPRESENTATIVE IN CONGRESS FROM THE STATE OF PENNSYLVANIA

Mr. RIDGE. It is a pleasure and a privilege to appear before you today, particularly with Jan Scruggs, the director of the Vietnam Veterans Memorial Fund, and, hopefully, our colleague and friend, David Bonior.

I don't think there is any truth to the rumor that he is not here because he is undecided on NAFTA and down at the White House. But his commitment and his effort on promoting this bill and getting over 300 cosponsors demonstrate, frankly, the same kind of energy he is bringing to that debate as well. So I am pleased to be testifying with him, even if it is in absentia for the time being.

I would like to strongly urge the subcommittee to pass H.R. 1608, the 1994 Vietnam Veterans Memorial Commemorative Coin Act. It is appropriate that a hearing to consider this measure be held on the eve of the day set aside to honor those that have served this country, and on the eve of a wonderful and long-overdue addition to the Vietnam Wall to recognize the women who served so bravely during that war. Veterans Day is only one of the many ways that America demonstrates the debt of gratitude it owes to protect its principles.

The legislation that David Bonior and I have introduced would require that the Secretary of the Treasury mint coins to commemorate the 10th anniversary of the Vietnam Veterans Memorial. This is a bipartisan bill, cosponsored by over 300 of our colleagues, including a majority from the Banking Committee. I strongly believe that the Vietnam Veterans Memorial, often referred to as The Wall, is deserving of such commemoration and support.

The Vietnam war was the longest war in the history of our Nation, lasting from July 1957 to May 1975. Each of the over 2,500,000 men and women who served the military in Vietnam endured a unique experience, and each remembers in an individual and personal way that experience 20 years later, myself included.

The Wall welds these experiences together to remind all Americans of what can be lost when a country goes to war. It is a unique and powerful tribute to the over 58,000 men and women that died in service to their country, and a reminder to all Americans that there are still over 2,200 persons listed as missing in action.

A coin commemorating the Vietnam Veterans Memorial will once again recognize these brave warriors and the ultimate sacrifices they have made for their country, and will pay special tribute to those who wore the country's uniform during the Vietnam era. This recognition of Vietnam veterans is not only deserving, but it is also appropriate.

I know among the committee members there is some concern that legislation has already been passed to authorize a coin program for the World Cup in 1994. And that there is a concern that passing legislation to mint coins to commemorate the Vietnam Memorial in 1994 will flood the numismatic community and jeopardize both of these laudable coin programs. However, we believe the market for the Vietnam Memorial Commemorative coin will reach far, far beyond those that would ordinarily participate in coin collection.

The Wall is the most visited memorial in the United States. It draws over 2.5 million visitors annually. These visitors do not leave without being personally and emotionally affected, because they are remembering the loss of a loved one, remembering their own experience in Vietnam and friends that did not return, or because the memorial is a stark reminder to all who visit of the personal sacrifice borne by those called upon to serve their country and the sacrifice made by their families and communities.

Madam Chairwoman, these are the people that will purchase this coin.

It is appropriate that we authorize the Secretary of the Treasury to mint these coins in 1994, because it will be the 10th anniversary of the addition of Frederick Hart's 7-foot bronze statute, The Three Serviceman and a flagpole at the Memorial. It will also be the 10th anniversary, 10 years since the Vietnam Veterans Memorial Fund gave the Memorial to the U.S. Government. The VVMF did retain certain rights and responsibilities and I believe Jan Scruggs will address some of those later.

Through issuing a half a million coins, the legislation will raise approximately $5 million to endow the Memorial permanently, and I think that it is very important, to endow this Memorial permanently. This bill is revenue neutral and will ultimately represent a savings to the government as it precludes, because of the permanent endowment, the need for any future appropriation from the government to repair The Wall.

Once again, I thank the subcommittee for the opportunity to testify on behalf of H.R. 1608, and ask that you report to the full committee as expeditiously as possible.

[The prepared statement of Mr. Thomas Ridge can be found in the appendix.]

Mr. FIELDS [presiding]. Any questions from members of the subcommittee?

I would like to ask Mr. Eugene Essner to please step forward and be seated at the table.

Mr. Essner is the Deputy Director for the U.S. Mint. He is a Senior Executive Service employee with 29 years of experience. This afternoon he is going to discuss the coin issue. Please proceed as you see fit.

## STATEMENT OF EUGENE H. ESSNER, DEPUTY DIRECTOR U.S. MINT

Mr. ESSNER. Thank you, Mr. Chairman. Good afternoon, Mr. Chairman and members of the subcommittee. Thank you for the opportunity to express the views of the Treasury Department concerning the following commemorative coin bills: H.R. 535, the Prisoner of War Commemorative Coin Act; H.R. 789, the Jefferson Commemorative Coin Act of 1993; H.R. 1608, the 1994 Vietnam Veterans Memorial Commemorative Coin Act; and H.R. 1697, the Women in Military Service for America Memorial Commemorative Coin Act.

H.R. 535 mandates the issuance of not more than 1.5 million silver coins for the period of January 15, 1994 through December 31, 1994 in honor of Americans who have been prisoners of war. The Jefferson bill, H.R. 789, commemorates the 250th anniversary of the birth of Thomas Jefferson with the minting of not more than 600,000 silver coins from July 4, 1993 through July 4, 1994. The Vietnam Veterans Memorial bill, H.R. 1608, requires the production of not more than 500,000 silver coins in commemoration of the 10th anniversary of the Memorial for the period of April 1, 1994 through April 1, 1995. Last, H.R. 1697 commemorates American women who have served in the military with the issuance of not more than 50,000 gold and 500,000 silver coins, beginning on November 1, 1993 and ending on December 31, 1994.

As you know, on May 27, 1993, the Senate passed S. 50, the Senate companion bill to H.R. 789, the Jefferson bill; and on September 21, 1993, the Senate Banking Committee favorably reported out the companion bills of the three veteran bills under consideration here today.

The Department of the Treasury has been a consistent voice for limiting the growth of commemorative coin programs. We often find ourselves in the unenviable position of being torn between worthwhile and sympathetic causes and events for which a group is seeking commemoration, and the need to avoid saturating the commemorative coin market. This is another such occasion.

The Department of the Treasury opposes these bills as currently drafted. This opposition is not because of any belief that the subject matter of the coins is inappropriate, but rather to protect the commemorative coin market as a whole. If Congress nonetheless chooses to authorize another commemorative Coin bill for 1994, we believe that the most viable option would be to consolidate the three bills that commemorate veterans groups. Properly structured, one coin program, with the proceeds divided among the sponsoring organizations, would increase chances of success for all the sponsoring organizations.

While we have no objection to the merits of the Thomas Jefferson coin legislation, we are concerned over having at least three coin programs in 1994, and perhaps as many as five. We urge that this bill be submitted to the Citizens Commemorative Coin Advisory Committee for a recommendation on timing.

Since the early 1980's, Congress has authorized 18 commemorative coin programs. Two of the already authorized programs for 1994 through 1996 are among the largest programs ever undertaken by the mint. The 1994 World Cup Program authorizes the issuance of up to 10.75 million gold, silver, and clad coins. The 1995/1996 Olympic Program, the most ambitious ever launched, requires the issuance of 16 coins—4 gold coins, 8 silver coins, and 4 clad coins—during a 2-year period, for a total of up to 17.95 million coins.

In addition, the Civil War Coin Program authorizes up to 3.3 million gold, silver, and clad coins in 1995.

To put these ambitious programs in a larger context, only one of the dozen commemorative coin programs of the past 7 years has registered sales of 4 million coins. The Veterans Coin Programs and the Jefferson Program would be competing for marketing resources and limited collector disposable income with the already authorized programs, and with each other as well.

The enabling legislation for commemorative coin programs generally mandates that a portion of the coin sale proceeds, usually designated as surcharges, is to be paid to a designated recipient organization. Over $300 million in surcharges have been generated from mint commemorative coin sales since the 1984 Olympic Coin Program. Sales figures from the coin programs since 1986, however, reflect a declining interest in commemorative coins by the numismatic community, which constitutes about 90 percent of coin purchasers. The 1986 Statue of Liberty Commemorative Coin Program raised approximately $83 million in surcharges; the 1992 Olympic Program raised only $9 million.

We believe that it is critical that the number of commemorative coin programs be limited in order to stem the falling demand for commemorative coins, foster an effective secondary market, and ensure the success of future coin programs.

Numerous coin programs offered during the same time period compete with each other. This competition threatens the success of the individual programs and is likely to result in below-expectation sales for all of the programs. This was clearly apparent when the USO Commemorative Coin Program, which was the third program for 1991, had very low sales relative to the first two programs of that year.

We fully recognize, however, that these concerns cannot easily reverse the current tide of commemorative coinage, especially when there are so many worthwhile causes supported by these programs. Congress has begun to address this problem with its enactment of legislation establishing the Citizens Commemorative Coin Advisory Committee. The key purpose of the committee, which was created in response to concern over the growing proliferation of commemorative coin bills, is to provide advice to Congress on the selection of subjects for commemorative coins.

For your information, we are in the final stages of setting up the committee. After soliciting nominations for membership through the *Federal Register* and the media, receiving applications, and reviewing approximately 80 resumes and conducting interviews, we are ready to make final recommendations to the Secretary of the Treasury. The committee should be fully operational before the end of this year, and we hope it will be instrumental in exacting greater control over the number of bills enacted.

In the interim, if legislation is to be enacted, the mint proposes that the three veterans bills be converted from separate, competing programs to a consolidated commemorative coin program. A merger would allow all of the designated recipient organizations to benefit from the collection of surcharges from a three-coin series. We believe that one combined program would be more successful and more efficiently marketed and managed than multiple programs offered during the same time period.

We recommend that an omnibus veterans coin bill be drafted to provide the mint maximum flexibility to structure a highly marketable coin program. We also recommend that the bill provide for low mintage levels and limited availability of the coins. Reduced mintage levels would increase total revenue for designated recipients. A combined program would also allow us to better dedicate resources to the project. To this end, we would be happy to work with the subcommittee to develop alternative legislation.

If, however, the bills go forward as currently drafted, we have the following technical comments.

The starting date proposed in the Jefferson bill was this past July, and we seriously questioned whether the mint could effectively, if at all, produce and market this coin program by its completion date of July 1994. Moreover, it is simply not practical to set the starting dates for this month and January 1994 as proposed by H.R. 1697 and H.R. 535, respectively. It generally takes at least 6 months from passage of legislation to the beginning of coin production. Leadtime is required by the mint to select designs, produce dies, conduct trial strikes, procure boxes, and so forth.

We also believe that the total number of silver coins offered in each commemorative coin program should be restricted to 500,000 coins.

H.R. 535, the POW bill, calls for a mintage level of 1.5 million silver coins. This amount is simply too high to ensure collector interest. Setting the maximum mintage at a level slightly below sales projections generates greater interest in a coin program by developing a secondary market and actually increases demand for the coin and the surcharges that can be collected.

For example, the 1992 White House Commemorative Coin Program offered a silver coin with a maximum mintage level of only 500,000 coins for a single-year program. All coins sold out in less than 3 weeks, and the value of these coins has increased since the sellout.

H.R. 535 also requires the funding mechanism for the program to be the Coinage Profit Fund, which is no longer being used for commemorative coin programs. The Numismatic Public Enterprise Fund is the proper funding source.

Last, two of the veterans bills, H.R. 535 and H.R. 1697, call for the coins to bear a 1993 date, rather than 1994, the year the coins would be issued. Experience has shown us that the collectors prefer commemorative coins which are offered and inscribed with the current year's date. The Jefferson bill, H.R. 789, also mandates a 1993 dated coin, since 1993 is the 250th anniversary of the birth of Jefferson. While we realize the significance of using 1993, the same numismatic concerns would apply.

Thank you again for convening this hearing and for giving us the opportunity to share with the subcommittee the Treasury Department's views on these bills specifically and on commemorative coinage in general.

Thank you, Mr. Chairman.

[The prepared statement of Mr. Essner can be found in the appendix.]

Mr. FIELDS. The written statements for the rest of our proceedings all will be submitted for the record.

Any questions from members of the panel?

Ms. Waters from California.

Ms. WATERS. Thank you very much, Mr. Chairman.

I heard what you are recommending, combining the three coins in order to lessen the competition somewhat, but I didn't understand how that would work. If you combined H.R. 535, H.R. 1608 and H.R. 1697, I guess, you would have gold, silver, and what?

Mr. ESSNER. No, Madam Congresswoman. We would propose that we have a three silver dollar series of 500,000 each. That would be a total of 1.5 million silver dollars, but there would be three different designs, with the maximum limit of 500,000 each.

Ms. WATERS. All right. I would like to know, how many commemorative coins do you have for and about the subject of women?

Mr. ESSNER. I am sorry?

Ms. WATERS. Women. How many coins do you have in the history of coinage that commemorate anything about women?

Mr. ESSNER. I don't have an exact answer; I do know that on one of our recent commemorative coins we did—it was a military—one of the military-related coins we did, I believe, included a woman on the coin. I would have to check that to make sure.

I know in some of the older coins there were some women, or at least depictions of Liberty as a woman, but I am not sure of any specific number.

Ms. WATERS. Would you please, if you don't mind, Mr. Essner, see if you can get a little historical data for me so that I can understand what our efforts have been directed to, for and about women. I would appreciate that very much.

Mr. ESSNER. We will be happy to provide that.

[The information referred to can be found in the appendix.]

Ms. WATERS. I think I had one other question that I would like to ask you. Did you take into consideration—you seem to have an awful lot of information that helps you to conclude about the potential success of these coins. Evidently, that is information that has been gathered over a long period of time, and perhaps you have some other information that allows you to do the kind of projections that you just did.

I would like to know, in all of that information, do you have anything that shows interest by the majority of our citizens, women, and the support for a coin that would specifically commemorate the role of women in the military or in anything else?

If not, is it something that maybe you could conclude as you study the projections about the potential success? Because I think that you may find that you may have an interest that you have not considered in the past.

Mr. ESSNER. We would be happy to take a look at that.

Generally, what we would do is use focus groups to determine levels of interest. We have not, obviously, done any focus groups on these particular coins, because they have not been legislated yet, and we do not normally do research on the bills until we are ready to present testimony.

But even at that point, we haven't done research using our marketing agencies, but we could certainly take a look at that.

Ms. WATERS. Wouldn't that be helpful in making a determination about whether or not all of the coins should be grouped together or whether or not you find something that is so new and interesting that you would want to say, well, I think this coin may do well on its own?

Mr. ESSNER. Well, I think in general terms, absolutely yes. But in most cases, we are directed by the Congress on the passage of coins, and then we react to that. We are not the ones who generally determine what coins would be the best coins to be issued, or which would be the most saleable.

We do sometimes give our opinions to Congressmen on specific coins, but we react to the direction of the Congress. And at that point, it is not a matter of whether we do the coin or not; it is how much we can sell.

Ms. WATERS. Yes. I was interested in the very sound testimony that you gave today, because as you know, that testimony influences Members and the direction that they want to go in.

I know you want to give the best and most complete information that you can give. If you are to do that, perhaps it would be worthwhile to take a look at this new phenomenon, the purchasing power of women, in order to factor that into the recommendations that you make to Congress, so that we can make the best decision.

Would that not be something that you could do?

Mr. ESSNER. We could certainly have a marketing agency look at that, yes.

Ms. WATERS. All right. Thank you very much.

Mr. FIELDS. The gentleman from California.

Mr. MCCANDLESS. Thank you, Mr. Chairman.

Mr. Essner, will you go back over the history of the Citizens Commemorative Coin Advisory Committee? You mentioned that in your comments. Having been on this subcommittee at the time, I think it would be better if the subcommittee saw it through your eyes, rather than mine, in how this evolved during the 102d Congress.

Mr. ESSNER. Well, Mr. Congressman, I think, to the best of my recollection, it was an attempt to try to get some control on the number of commemorative coins that would be issued and on the subjects that would be commemorated. Over the past 10 years, particularly in the latter part of this time, the number of commemorative coins that are being proposed has increased dramatically, and we have been expressing more concern about the proliferation of the coins. So the attempt was to, or I believe the intent of the Congress was to establish this committee which would be providing annual reports to the Congress recommending a 5-year projection of the events which they feel are worthy of having commemorative coins issued.

Mr. MCCANDLESS. We constructed for the subcommittee and made available, I believe to all members, this chart which illustrates the success or lack thereof of commemorative coins.

Maybe you have seen this, Mr. Essner?

Mr. ESSNER. No, I have not.

73-932 O - 94 - 2

Mr. McCANDLESS. What it simply shows is the level at which the commemorative coins were authorized versus the actual sales. And, of course, this is extremely important when you are developing a commemorative coin program, particularly if you are betting on a certain amount of money for an endowment or for some type of activity that would result from the sale of those coins.

And this is why it became important, then, that we try to establish some reasonable way of having a coin program reflect what is most productive and what is most desirable, and however else you wish to explain it, in the way of a commemorative coin program.

The problem that this subcommittee has had in the past is that each member is subjected to another member who wants a commemorative coin program, and so at the end of a given period of time, you have requests on the part of 15 or 20—even more sometimes—people who want a commemorative coin.

Over a period of time, it was established by those who preceded me that one of the thresholds would be a discharge petition with 218 signatures as the beginning point, of Members of Congress, which slowed down the proliferation to a certain degree, but I don't think it totally addresses the problem. So as Mr. Essner has said, it was the desire of the last Congress that this advisory committee be formed for the purpose of developing criteria that would be separate from the human emotions of someone doing something for a friend.

And this is certainly in no way to take away from the value of the subject matter of these coins, but to try to make some sense out of it and to give it an objective direction rather than somewhat of a subjective direction.

I felt that this was necessary at this point, because this has become a rather interesting subject relative to this subcommittee.

Thank you, Mr. Chairman.

Mr. FIELDS. The gentleman from Georgia.

Mr. LINDER. Thank you, Mr. Chairman.

Mr. Essner, has there been any effort to, or would it be possible to, quantify the dilution factor in each of these programs because of the numbers of programs up for sale at one time? It appears over the last 10 years from these numbers that regardless of how many coins were minted, the market—the purchasing market is only 2, 3 million people—or 2, 3 million coins.

Mr. ESSNER. Yes, Mr. Congressman. I think I would reach the same conclusion. I would say, however, we do not mint the number of coins that are authorized. One of the things that we do is we start marketing the coins, and then we scale our mintage to what we are able to sell.

So I don't want to give you the impression that we have minted all of these coins and are now melting them down. Because whatever is left at the end of the program, we do melt down.

That is really important to the collecting community also, because they want their coins to have a value. And if we were later to dump these coins into the marketplace, the value would drop on the existing coins.

But, yes, it seems as though you could authorize a coin with 50 million—a 50 million authorized level; and it doesn't mean we would sell a single additional coin than if you authorized it at 2 million or 1 million.

I think that goes back to my testimony where I said about 90 percent of the coin sales on any of these programs are sold through our collectors' list. I mean no offense to any of the organizations, but we have heard over the years, that "our" coin program will be different. They claim to have the constituents out there that will buy these coins, and invariably that just doesn't prove to be the fact. It is the coin collectors who are the primary purchasers of the coins.

Mr. LINDER. And you know who they are.

Mr. ESSNER. Most of them are on a mailing list that we have, about 2 million people.

Mr. LINDER. That is a finite number?

Mr. ESSNER. It changes.

During the Statue of Liberty Coin Program, which was certainly the most successful coin program that we have ever had, we added a number of people to our mailing list. Many of those people were not true collectors however, and after a few years, they dropped off. And after a few years, it is no longer profitable for us to keep them on our mailing list. We were just spending more money and not getting any results. So they have dropped off. So the list changes.

Mr. LINDER. Have there been periods of time recently when there have been several competing coins out there?

Mr. ESSNER. Yes. In fact, last year in 1992, we had three competing coin programs. We had the White House Coin Program, 1992 Olympic Coin Program, and the Christopher Columbus Coin Program. Three coin programs in the same year.

In 1993 we have the James Madison Coin Program, and the World War II Coin Program.

Mr. LINDER. And if you put those programs together, it appears that there is still the same number of coins sold cumulatively? Roughly?

Mr. ESSNER. Roughly, yes.

Mr. LINDER. So if one coin was out there that could possibly sell 2.5 to 3 million coins on its own, but if you put 3 or 4 coin programs out there, it is going to be 2 to 3 million coins cumulative?

Mr. ESSNER. I wouldn't say the numbers are that high. But——

Mr. LINDER. In general terms.

Mr. ESSNER. They do definitely compete and feed off of one another, yes.

Mr. LINDER. So is it reasonable to extrapolate that information and say that all of these programs would be doing better if there was some kind of timing mechanism and they weren't all competing with each other?

Mr. ESSNER. Yes, I would think that—I would certainly think that is true. But I also think it is important that we keep the mintage levels for each program at a low enough level. We like to say that we want to keep everybody wanting a little bit.

If you set the mintage at 600,000 and you sell 575,000, then you have to pretty much assume that everybody that wanted one of the coins got one. In the White House coin, where the mintage level was set at 500,000, we sold out in just a few weeks. The demand was still there, that sparked the interest in the numismatic community and the price went up on the secondary market, which is something that these people are looking for and it increases the interest in all of our numismatic coin programs.

Mr. LINDER. How many of these programs have had international appeal?

Mr. ESSNER. Well, certainly the 1983, 1984 Olympic Coin Program did.

The Statue of Liberty Coin Program did.

I think following that, simply because on the Statue of Liberty, we were so successful—and that was another issue where there were only 500,000 gold coins, and it was the first quarter ounce gold coin issued since the 1930's. The price went up on the secondary market.

Then when we followed on with the Constitution Coin Program, there was also interest from the international marketplace, I think primarily as an investment. But that investment didn't prove out to be a very good investment. And after that, our international interest dropped off significantly.

If I can go over the programs; 1988 Olympics, there was very little international interest. In fact, we had objections from the Korean Government because we were not the host country of the Olympics. And I think the Japanese refused to allow us to even send the coins into Japan, because they felt they should be supporting Korea, who was the host country.

The Congress coin I think there was very little interest in internationally.

Ms. WATERS. I don't blame them.

Mr. ESSNER. No offense.

Eisenhower, again a small amount.

Mount Rushmore, not a lot.

The Korean coin, I will compliment, he is deceased now, General Stillwell. He personally took it upon himself to make trips to Korea and promoted the coins into the international market. So we did get some sales there. Not a lot.

Mr. MCCANDLESS. If the gentleman would yield.

Mr. LINDER. I would be happy to yield.

Mr. MCCANDLESS. Just as an example, for those who have hair turning the color of mine, the USO came to us, and said anybody who has ever been to a USO will buy a USO coin. Having been to the USO in World War II and then again being recalled in Korea, I said, yes, it sounds like a pretty good story to me. So we authorized 1 million silver dollars, if I remember correctly, if my information is correct; and we sold 446,233. An example of what one would consider to be a very popular subject for a commemorative coin.

I think the problem there probably centers around the fact that everybody assumed that it would sell itself, and it didn't.

Conversely, in the case of General——

Mr. ESSNER. Stillwell.

Mr. MCCANDLESS. Stillwell. Thank you. And the Korean coin, that was a project whose time had come for the purpose of developing what is necessary in the way of a foundation for the Memorial, and you had a group of people who are out there merchandizing beyond that of the normal activities of the mint.

So it takes an organization to sell these coins. They just don't sell themselves.

Mr. LINDER. Let me just close by saying I have a private interest here. Representing Atlanta, Georgia, I have a keen interest in the Olympics; and that program is already in position.

I am convinced that some of these programs will dilute the interest in that, and we believe could reduce the revenues by as much as 20 percent.

Having said that, I also was a volunteer in the military in the Air Force during Vietnam, and I go to that Wall and see my friends' names on it. And I was one of the originators of activity in the 1970's on behalf of POWs. I am a sponsor on virtually all of these coins.

But I think it would enhance the value of each program if we would find some way to put these requests in the hands of the Commission to find some way to bring them out on schedules that would not compete with each other and enhance the value of each program. I think that is what I hear you say, and I think I would support that.

Thank you, Mr. Chairman.

Mr. FIELDS. The gentlewoman from California?

Ms. WATERS. Would you describe the Commission to me again, Mr. Essner?

Mr. ESSNER. The Advisory Committee was established last year. It consists of one representative from the U.S. Mint, three representatives from the numismatic or arts or museum community, and three members from the general public.

And they are to meet and provide a report annually. I believe it is annually.

Ms. WATERS. Who appoints these people?

Mr. ESSNER. I am sorry.

Ms. WATERS. Who appoints the members?

Mr. ESSNER. The Secretary of the Treasury.

And it makes recommendations to the Congress, basically to have a 5-year plan—out 5 years as to what they would recommend would be commemorated during that period of time. And this would be updated each year adding 1 new year.

Ms. WATERS. And one last question: Do we always have a request for the Olympics and the World Cup? Is that consistent?

Mr. ESSNER. Well, this is the first time the United States has hosted the World Cup, and I am told, at least, that in our lifetime, it will probably not host the World Cup again. It moves around the world.

But the Olympics, yes, the 1984 Olympics, when it was held in Los Angeles, we raised $73 million to help the USOC and the LAOOC.

They have then requested and obtained a program in 1988 and 1992; and, now again, it has been passed for the 1996 hosting in Atlanta.

Now, certainly we know, of course, that the Atlanta Coin Program, the 1996 program will be immensely more successful than the 1992 and 1988 programs.

Ms. WATERS. How do you know?

Mr. ESSNER. Well, simply because we are the host country. And that is one of the things that people from other countries are interested in. They want to collect the coins of the host country. That is one reason our sales in the international marketplace during 1988 and 1992 were very small.

Mr. MCCANDLESS. If the gentlelady would yield, one of the strong proponents of the World Cup coin was our subcommittee chairman, Mr. Torres. And part of the World Cup activities will take place in Los Angeles.

Ms. WATERS. That is fine. I just suspect that there are those events that will be consistent. It seems that the Olympics has taken a place in the coinage world and for every Olympics, there will probably be a coin and there probably will not be a lot of objections to it.

And when you have something that appears to have support, for whatever reason, you are putting everything else in the position of having to compete with it. However, since we are going to have an advisory committee, and I guess that advisory committee is going to be taken seriously in these decisions as we view their recommendations, perhaps we will have a way to make arguments on behalf of coins that perhaps cannot compete as easily with something that is growing into a tradition, like the Olympics.

And perhaps we will also have an opportunity to help make sure that the Secretary for now or for the future identify an advisory board that will take into consideration many of the concerns perhaps that have not been taken into consideration before. Thank you.

Mr. ESSNER. Thank you.

Mr. FIELDS. There being no further questions, we want to thank you very much, sir, for your testimony today.

Mr. ESSNER. Thank you.

Mr. FIELDS. The next witness is Brig. Gen. Wilma Vaught, the U.S. Air Force [retired]. She is the president of the board of directors of the Women in Military Service for the American Memorial Foundation. Her last military assignment was commander of the U.S. Military Entrance Process and Command in Chicago, Illinois, where she served from June 1982 until she retired in August 1985. General Vaught is one of the most decorated military women in our U.S. history.

General Vaught, it is a pleasure to have you before the subcommittee today; your written testimony will be accepted for the record, so you can proceed, and we are going to give you 5 minutes to proceed in any way you wish to. You may proceed.

## STATEMENT OF WILMA VAUGHT, PRESIDENT, WOMEN IN MILITARY SERVICE MEMORIAL FOUNDATION

General VAUGHT. Mr. Chairman and members of the subcommittee, on behalf of our women service members, past and present, their families and supporters, I deeply appreciate this opportunity to speak to the merits of the Women in Military Service Memorial Commemorative Coin bill.

First, I want to emphasize that this is far more than just another coin bill. This bill will do two critical things: First, it will commemorate and honor the 1.8 million women who have served our country and who serve it today.

We understand that there is this idea of lumping this bill with other bills being proposed. Let me explain why it is important that this not be done in this case. We are recognizing service, women's service, which began with the Revolutionary War and spans time through today. Our mandate for the Memorial is to honor women. These coins and the Memorial they benefit are not oriented to a specific conflict or event as most coins have been, such as the Korean war and World War II.

The coins themselves will appeal to a different audience, women veterans and women who don't ordinarily buy coins as well as veterans and coin dealers. They must be marketed differently than other coins to reach that audience. A key aspect of the marketing strategy to be successful has to be an appeal to all women. Lumping them into a veterans package as proposed loses that marketing angle and severely depletes the potential market within and beyond the ordinary collectors.

Second, this Coin bill is about building this memorial right here. The women's memorial will give the long overdue permanent recognition our military women have earned. Proceeds with the coin sale will provide the final increment of funds needed to build. We need these funds so that we can start construction in 1994. All funds received will be used in constructing and furnishing the Memorial, and that alone.

I want to stress, this memorial honors all the women who served in war and those who served during times of peace. They have overcome harassment, discrimination, and barriers. They have been in ships which were torpedoed, been bombed and strafed, been POWs, typed orders, repaired airplanes and flown them. They have earned their own memorial; they deserve their own coin.

It is interesting to note that although women's military service began with the American Revolution and continued through every major war and conflict, it was not until Operation Desert Storm that as a nation we finally verbally recognized this fact and referred to our troops as the men and women serving in Desert Storm, rather than just our boys over there or our men.

Dating back to the 1800's, only three coins have depicted women alone: 1893, Queen Isabella of Spain; 1937, Elinor Dare and her baby from the Lost Colony. In 1979, Susan B. Anthony. And in the present World War II commemorative coin, there is one coin which depicts three men and one woman. Surely, it is not too much to ask that a fourth mintage be authorized specifically to honor the 1.8 million women service members who stepped forward as volunteers time after time and risked or lost their lives for their country just as our men did.

The minting of coins has been authorized in recognition of everything from our forefathers to sports events. Surely, 1.8 million women can have their own coin. The U.S. Congress has said that it is worth building a memorial to honor our military women. Surely this subcommittee will now say that it is worth authorizing the gold and silver coins proposed to recognize the contributions of our women and their dedication, sacrifice, and commitment and to bring about the completion of the women's memorial.

I would ask you to note that the Memorial project includes the repair and restoration of the sorely neglected main entrance to the Arlington National Cemetery, the site of the Memorial in our Nation's most hallowed resting place.

Consider the fact that this bill and the Memorial has the full support of the veteran community, the American Nursing Association, and the major women's organizations.

As you deliberate about H.R. 1697, I ask you to think of these coins and this memorial and they are to honor women like those here today. Dorothy Jefferson behind me; Laura Brown, who served in the Pacific for 2½ years in World War II, both of them are World War II veterans and charter members of the Memorial. Margaret Duvall, whose sister served in World War II and her daughter served in Vietnam. Frances Crawford is a Vietnam era veteran. Jessie Bledsoe who also served in World War II.

Members of the foundation board are here: Brig. Gen. Connie Slewitzke, the vice president, former chief of the Army Nurse Corps who served in Vietnam; Brig. Gen. Sally Wells, former chief of the Army—or the Air Force Nurse Corps and a flight nurse who flew med evac missions bringing back the wounded from Vietnam; Col. Sally Pritchett, the U.S. Marine Corps [retired]; Chief Officer Betty Splaine, U.S. Coast Guard [retired], the first woman to be promoted to warrant officer in the Coast Guard; Command Sgt. Maj. Mildred Kelly, U.S. Army [retired].

They all came because they care about this bill and the Memorial. They are just a few of the people this bill and this Memorial are important to. We urge you to approve H.R. 1697 as it stands.

I can't believe you would want to send a message across the country that women's roles in the building and protection of this Nation will continue to go unrecognized and undervalued. I firmly believe that the record of the experiences of the 1.8 million women the Memorial will tell about have to be considered important. I know they will enrich the lives of not only America's service women and women veterans, but women in every Nation, because all of us can share in the pride and heritage and accomplishments of those who paved the way.

Just a few weeks ago, a woman came unannounced to our office with her daughter, granddaughter, and great-granddaughter. She served as a Navy yeoman in World War I. At age 94, she stood straight and showed us her I.D. card and said I have carried this with me everywhere I have gone for 75 years. I want to see this Memorial built now. We won't be forgotten. Don't forget these ladies.

[The prepared statement of General Vaught can be found in the appendix.]

Mr. FIELDS. That concludes your opening remarks. We are going to recess just for a few moments. There is a vote taking place on the floor, so we are going to—I am going to recognize the gentlewoman from California.

Ms. WATERS. I am sorry, I will not be coming back and I wanted to have an opportunity to thank you for all of the work that you have done on behalf of the Memorial, and all of the women who are here today.

I am a little bit tired today, and so I am going to be very careful about what I say, except to tell you that this is going to emerge as an important issue in this Congress. I will go to the Women's caucus. I am going to ask the Women's caucus of Congress to get behind this and to give full support to it.

I don't care what they say about the Olympics, the USO or anything else. This is different, this is special, and it is important, and enough is enough.

Thank you very much.

Mr. FIELDS. The subcommittee is going to be in recess temporarily.

[Recess.]

Mr. FIELDS [presiding]. When we recessed, we had General Vaught giving her testimony. Have you concluded, General, your testimony?

General VAUGHT. Yes. I have finished. The only additional thing I would have said is that we stand ready to work with the subcommittee, the Mint, with the Department of the Treasury, to assure a successful program.

Mr. FIELDS. I want to thank you very much for your testimony. It will be noted for the record. There are no questions. So at this time we are going to ask the remaining witnesses to come forward, each of the remaining witnesses. If you would come forward, Mr. Jan Scruggs, Daniel Jordan, and Wayne Hitchcock.

Gentlemen, your testimony will be submitted for the record, your written testimony. We will start with you, Mr. Scruggs, if you would give your opening remarks, oral remarks, and then we will ask Mr. Jordan to follow and then Mr. Hitchcock.

## STATEMENT OF JAN SCRUGGS, PRESIDENT, VIETNAM VETERANS MEMORIAL FUND

Mr. SCRUGGS. My name is Jan Scruggs, I am president of the Vietnam Veterans Memorial Fund, the VVMF. I am appearing this afternoon testifying in support of H.R. 1608. This legislation, of course, would authorize minting of a commemorative coin, recognizing the Nation's most visited memorial, the Vietnam Veterans Memorial. What distinguishes this bill is that this legislation saves the government money.

The funds generated will take the place of money that the government would have to spend for the Memorial. Congress authorized the VVMF to build the Memorial on July 1, 1980. In November 1982, the Memorial was dedicated. In 1984, the Three Serviceman Statue was added along with the flagpole, and all of these elements were built by VVMF through private contributions which we raised from the American people. Tomorrow, of course, will be another addition, the statue representing the women who served in Vietnam.

In 1984, VVMF gave the Memorial to the U.S. Government. A Memorandum of Conveyance provided that the VVMF would continue significant stewardship duties. These duties include semiannual ceremonies, providing funds for repair, and restoration of the Memorial, providing funds in case of catastrophic damage to the Memorial and its various elements.

For the record, I will submit or give to the staff of the subcommittee the Memorandum of Conveyance signed by former President Reagan.

As part of our stewardship we have purchased eight granite panels and stored them in a secure location on the Quantico Marine Base. If the funding becomes available, VVMF would like to purchase enough granite so as to allow a complete replacement of the Memorial's walls. If this should ever be required, the granite would actually be cut, polished, and then put into place on outdoor frames where each panel would age and weather like the Memorial's walls are aging and weathering now. Although this might seem like an extraordinary precaution, we do believe that it is warranted under the circumstances that I will explain.

This unique Memorial has difficulties which indeed in turn are unique. Several of the Memorial's granite panels have developed cracks, and these cracks may simply be attributable to flaws in the granite and may be unlikely to worsen, or more ominously, may be caused by a controversial system of pins and anchors on a concrete wall behind the granite panels, a support system which may be placing destructive stress on all of the panels.

Nationally recognized experts have studied the matter and have provided us with contradictory conclusions. As a general matter, we have been advised to wait and see how much the cracking worsens. If it turns out that the panel support system is causing the cracking, VVMF will face the extraordinary expense of disassembling the Memorial, so that both the support system and the cracked panels can be replaced.

For the record, I will submit the status report on the current condition of the Vietnam Veterans Memorial prepared by an architect in June 1990 as well as the cause of cracking from the Vietnam Veterans Memorial. I will provide this to the staff of the subcommittee so that they will just have the information.

Chairman KENNEDY [presiding]. Without objection, so ordered.

[The information referred to can be found in the appendix.]

Mr. SCRUGGS. Apart from costs associated with the Memorial's walls, the extraordinary visitor traffic at the Memorial, many millions of people annually, this creates significant repair requirements that do need regular attention. For example, last year VVMF spent some $200,000 repairing the Memorial's granite walkways and correcting certain lighting problems. These maintenance costs which can be substantial will continue in the foreseeable future.

What are the Memorial's needs? I have mentioned a few. To provide an even more complete answer we are laying the groundwork for an expert study to be completed this summer giving VVMF an informed perspective about the projected problems over the next 100 years. Repairs to the Memorial, the statues, continuing to add names, walkways, replacing the directories of names, holders for the directories of names, also updating and changing the computerized system of names at the Memorial, helping the volunteer guides, and further walkways are examples of some of the projects necessary for future preservation of the Memorial.

Many have studied this Memorial to understand why the impact is so extraordinary. Why are Americans drawn to this wall of polished granite? These and many other questions continue to attract informed speculation.

But one thing is for certain. The Vietnam Veterans Memorial is a national treasure and the VVMF is committed to maintaining and preserving this memorial for future generations. Enacting H.R. 1608 would assure VVMF of the fiscal resources required to follow through on this commitment.

In closing, I want to thank the Chair of the subcommittee for the opportunity to appear in support of H.R. 1608. We believe that Congress would be able to take very great pride in the minting of a commemorative coin for the Memorial and that revenues generated from such a coin could be put to no more deserving purpose than to assure the future of the Nation's most visited memorial. And I might add, a symbol for our country just as important, as either the Lincoln or Jefferson Memorial.

And that concludes my testimony.

[The prepared statement of Mr. Scruggs can be found in the appendix.]

Chairman KENNEDY. Again, thank you very much. I apologize for not being here for all of your testimony, but we have talked in the past, and obviously you are one of the major reasons why we began moving on a lot of these coin bills. I thank you for all of the hard work you have done on behalf of Vietnam veterans and for veterans in general.

We appreciate your testimony today. Your full statement will be included in the record and any of the additional papers that you choose to submit will be accepted into the record.

Our next witness is Mr. Daniel Jordan, the executive director of the Thomas Jefferson Memorial Foundation.

Mr. Jordan, please proceed for 5 minutes.

## STATEMENT OF DANIEL P. JORDAN, EXECUTIVE DIRECTOR, THOMAS JEFFERSON MEMORIAL FOUNDATION

Mr. JORDAN. Thank you, Mr. Chairman, Mr. Fields. You have a copy of my statement for the record. In the interest of time, I will give a summary only.

Chairman KENNEDY. We appreciate that.

Mr. JORDAN. At the outset, however, because I feel somewhat outnumbered by these wonderful veterans in the Chamber, let me say that I did serve proudly in the U.S. Army infantry.

I am pleased to speak this afternoon on behalf of H.R. 789, which calls for the mintage of a Jefferson coin as part of the commemoration of the 250th anniversary of the man widely regarded as being the architect of American democracy.

I would add parenthetically that he was also the father of the American coinage system and a founder of the U.S. Mint.

The coin provides an opportunity not only to honor Mr. Jefferson, but also to inform all Americans about his life and ideals, and, in a tangible way, to perpetuate his legacy.

I believe the case for H.R. 789 is compelling. The Jefferson coin is timely and appropriate, and has broad appeal. It has overwhelming legislative support. It is written for a limited number of coins, and thus, it will not glut the market or cost the American taxpayers a penny. And finally, the Jefferson coin will provide badly needed help for Monticello, the home of Thomas Jefferson. I would like to elaborate a bit on that central point.

Monticello is a towering reminder of the Jeffersonian legacy; and Monticello needs, and we believe deserves, the public support that this coin would provide. This year Monticello will be visited by well over 600,000 individuals from all over the world. Twelve heads of State have come to Monticello in the past 3 years alone. The Clintons and Gores came on a cold Sunday morning in January, not only to kick off the 250th commemoration, but also to kick off their own inaugural and administration.

Monticello was ranked first in a recent national poll to determine America's favorite building, and Monticello is the only home in America on the World Heritage List, which is a United Nations compilation of international treasures that must be preserved at all costs. Monticello is the only American home on that list, which places us in the company with the Great Wall of China, the pyramids of Egypt, and the Taj Mahal. Monticello's future rests heavily on the Jefferson coin.

H.R. 789 will fund Monticello's first general endowment. And I want to emphasize that the money is entirely for that purpose—none of it will go for operating expenses. H.R. 789 will also advance our primary mission, which is preservation and education. The endowment will help support critical restoration work on the house itself, and we have several million dollars of projects ahead in that direction. Most of it, of course, we will pay for ourselves, but the endowment would be essential.

The endowment would also support the acquisition of Jefferson objects for display and for study. And I would note that we have a number of advisory panels in place to guide us in our work. We have one of museum professionals, another of prominent African-Americans, including Julian Bond, and several black scholars. The endowment will also help support a remarkable opportunity for global outreach through the newly established International Center for Jefferson Studies, which we are embarking upon as a collaborative scholarly venture with the University of Virginia, and with great support from the university and its president, John Casteen.

In conclusion, I strongly endorse H.R. 789 as an appropriate way for the Congress and Nation to recognize the 250th anniversary of the birth of perhaps America's greatest and most versatile statesman and in a manner that will provide lasting and tangible support for his legacy and memory.

I would add only, responding to a comment made by Mr. McCandless, that we would welcome the most stringent possible audit.

Thank you.

[The prepared statement of Mr. Jordan can be found in the appendix.]

Chairman KENNEDY. Thank you very much, Mr. Jordan.

I should have mentioned my thanks to Mr. Cleo Fields who is just an outstanding member of our subcommittee who has shown tremendous dedication to a broad array of issues that the subcommittee has addressed and I really appreciate his willingness to sit in as chairman. Just so long as you don't get too used to it there, Cleo. I appreciate it though, thank you.

Chairman KENNEDY. Our final witness of the day is Mr. Wayne Hitchcock who is the former national junior vice commander of the American Ex-Prisoners-of-War. It is a pleasure to have you here. Please proceed for 5 minutes.

## STATEMENT OF WAYNE HITCHCOCK, FORMER NATIONAL JUNIOR VICE COMMANDER, AMERICAN EX-PRISONERS-OF-WAR

Mr. HITCHCOCK. Thank you. Before I begin, I would like to introduce to you our commander, William Bearisto from the great State of Massachusetts. I think you are acquainted.

Chairman KENNEDY. I am very familiar with Bill and his beautiful wife who have come to my office on a whole range of issues, and are wonderful people.

Mr. HITCHCOCK. He is also accompanied by his wife and other members of our organization.

Mr. Chairman and Congressman Fields, American Ex-Prisoners-of-War are pleased to appear before you today seeking the support of H.R. 535, which would provide for the minting of coins in commemoration of Americans who were prisoners of war.

The profits derived from the sale of such a coin would be used for the purpose of building a museum at the Andersonville, Georgia, Civil War prison site. This national historic site is unique in the national park system as the only park to serve as a memorial to all Americans ever held prisoners of war.

The Congress stated the purpose of the park in the authorizing legislation, and I quote, to produce an understanding of the overall prisoner of war story of the Civil War, to interpret the role of prisoner of war camps in history, to commemorate the sacrifice of Americans who lost their lives in such camps, and to preserve the monuments located within that site, end of quote. Therefore, the need for a museum, within that site, to house the memorabilia of the former prisoner of war should be a first priority.

One hundred and forty-two thousand Americans were captured and interned as prisoner of war during World Wars I and II, Vietnam, and the Pueblo incident; 125,000 were returned to U.S. military control. Although the number of ex-prisoners of war are getting fewer, during the conflict in the Persian Gulf, 23 were captured and were immediately repatriated when the hostilities ceased, the latest of which we are presently very much aware of being Chief Warrant Officer Michael Durant who was shot down and captured in Somalia very recently.

As of January 1986, the Veterans' Administration records show that 83,000 former POWs were still alive. Latest statistics show that 66,000 alive as of January 1993. This is an average loss of almost 1,000 per year. This yearly loss can only increase rapidly as 116,000 of the total 142,000 were from World War II and now have an average age of 70 or more years, although we hate to admit it.

Therefore, time is of the essence to obtain our goal of the building of a museum at Andersonville in order to have a place for the prisoners of war story, their records, their history, and their memorabilia. Such a museum would therefore provide a place for all future generations to learn and recall the experiences of those who suffered as prisoners during the hostilities between nations.

How would the commemorative coin assist us? As stated in section 6(d) of H.R. 535, I quote, all sales of coins issued under this act would include a surcharge of $5 per coin. And in section 7(1), I quote, Secretary of Treasury shall make available to the Secretary of Interior the first $3 million for the construction of the Andersonville Prisoner of War Museum in Andersonville, Georgia, unquote. This amount would cover the cost to complete the Andersonville museum project.

There are presently 260 plus cosponsors on H.R. 535 and 54 cosponsors on companion bill S. 483. This bill passed the Senate Banking Committee on October 20 of this year and is presently on the Senate calendar. We might add that 1996 Olympics will be hosted in Georgia. This event will bring many visitors to Andersonville. This museum should be built prior to the Olympics. Construction is ready to start as soon as funds are available. Also, the community would be receptive to an entrance fee at the museum of $1, which would generate several hundred thousand dollars in revenue to the government.

In closing, let me repeat. For us, time is running out as age takes its toll. We need to start that museum today.

We thank this subcommittee for your deep-felt consideration in the passing of H.R. 535. And we would be happy to answer any questions that you might have.

[The prepared statement of Mr. Hitchcock can be found in the appendix.]

Chairman KENNEDY. Thank you very much, Mr. Hitchcock. I want to thank all of our witnesses for their informative testimony. These are not the kinds of issues that I think lend themselves to a great deal of examination in terms of questioning.

I want to say that we very much appreciate your coming in on short notice and providing us with your testimony today. We will be looking toward moving on these issues very, very shortly. I understand when I was not able to be present that there was some discussion of trying to bundle together some of these issues. We will be looking at those questions very, very carefully over the course of the next few days to make some determinations as to how to maximize the benefits to all of the competing interests, in light of the overwhelming evidence is that there is a relatively limited number of purchasers of coins.

While I know that some people might win and some people might lose under such a scheme, I want to look at what the merits of each individual coin are and make sure that we are not going to do something that will either hurt the overall efforts that are being made or hurt a particular effort, either. We will be looking to try to fashion some kind of reasonable way of proceeding.

I think that what we don't want to do, as I mentioned in my opening testimony, is kill the golden goose here. If we are told by the experts that by minting too many coins at one given time we are going to end up actually devaluing everybody's coin no one will benefit. I want to say this while you are here. I don't want you to leave and then have you feel that I was doing something without being straightforward with you about what my concerns are.

We can't have everybody say, "well, listen, I can sell more coins than the other guy." If that were to happen, the Mint will come in and say to me look, Joe, that is great, they all think they are going to be successful, but the reality is that there are only 1½ million people that are going to buy these coins even though people think they are going to be able to sell a lot more.

The whole history of these coins is that people think they are always going to do well; they don't. They end up not being able to be sold. If I wasn't strong enough and was a yes-man to everybody we would end up minting all of these individual coins which would not be bought. What you would then find is that the bottom falls out of the market and nobody can sell them because the coin collecting community just gets overrun with them.

I want you to know I understand that there is going to be a conflict. I don't know exactly how to resolve the conflict as we speak this afternoon. But we are going to have to work out some kind of compromise.

I don't know that everybody is going to be ecstatic over whatever it is that is worked out, but I pledge to you the fact that as chairman of this subcommittee, I will be working to try to maximize the number of dollars that end up flowing to the organizations that the Congress approves for these bills. I am not going to be taking sides on any particular effort.

What I will be doing is trying to make certain that we provide for the long-term health of the commemorative coin program, and that we don't do anything to hurt any particular effort that is being undertaken.

Cleo, do you have any thoughts that you would like to share?

Mr. FIELDS. No. I would just like to ditto your thoughts and your concerns. I have the same concerns. I do not want to take any particular sides, but would like to maximize the net share to each of the organizations. So that is my concern, and I have enjoyed the testimony from each, including the General.

I have enjoyed all of the testimony today and I have learned more about coins than I thought I would ever want to know. So I want to thank each of you for your testimony.

Chairman KENNEDY. Thank you all very, very much for your testimony. There being no further questions, on behalf of the subcommittee, I want to express my appreciation to all of the witnesses.

I would like to ask unanimous consent that the record be kept open for 4 weeks so that additional views may be submitted.

Let me also say that I look forward to hearing the views of the Commemorative Coin Commission and intend to give those views serious attention. Hearing no objection, it is so ordered.

The panel is excused and the subcommittee is in recess. Thank you for coming.

[Whereupon, at 5:20 p.m., the hearing was adjourned.]

# APPENDIX

November 10, 1993

73-932 O - 94 - 3

PREPARED STATEMENT OF HON. JOSEPH P. KENNEDY, II

NOVEMBER 10, 1993 COINAGE BILL HEARING -- OPENING STATEMENT

THE SUBCOMMITTEE WILL COME TO ORDER.

THIS AFTERNOON, THE SUBCOMMITTEE CONSIDERS FOUR PROPOSALS TO ESTABLISH COMMEMORATIVE COIN PROGRAMS. THEY ARE: FIRST, H.R. 535, THE PRISONER OF WAR COIN ACT; H.R. 789, THE JEFFERSON COIN ACT; H.R. 1608, THE VIETNAM VETERANS MEMORIAL COIN ACT; AND H.R. 1697, THE WOMEN IN MILITARY SERVICE COIN ACT. EACH OF THESE BILLS HAS OVER 218 CO-SPONSORS, AS REQUIRED BY THE RULES OF THE COMMITTEE TO HOLD A HEARING. I MIGHT ADD THAT, AS OF TODAY, THESE ARE THE ONLY COIN BILLS IN THE HOUSE WITH THE REQUISITE NUMBER OF COSPONSORS.

EACH OF THESE BILLS ALSO FURTHERS A VERY WORTHY CAUSE. I LOOK FORWARD TO HEARING FROM THEIR DISTINGUISHED AUTHORS SHORTLY.

THE CONSTITUTION GRANTS TO CONGRESS THE POWER TO MINT COINS. THE RULES OF THE HOUSE AND OF THE COMMITTEE INVEST THAT POWER IN THIS SUBCOMMITTEE. DURING MY BRIEF TENURE AS CHAIRMAN OF THIS SUBCOMMITTEE, I HAVE LEARNED MORE ABOUT COINAGE ISSUES THAN I EVER THOUGHT POSSIBLE. SEVERAL TRUTHS HAVE BECOME APPARENT:

FIRST, THERE HAS BEEN A PROLIFERATION OF COIN PROPOSALS IN THE CONGRESS IN RECENT YEARS. MANY OF THEM, INCLUDING THE ONES BEFORE US TODAY, HAVE GREAT MERIT; OTHERS DO NOT.

SECOND, COIN PROGRAMS CAN RAISE A GREAT DEAL OF MONEY FOR THE CAUSES THEY ARE EARMARKED TO FUND. OFTEN, THEY RAISE MORE MONEY THAN COULD BE FOUND BY THE NORMAL APPROPRIATIONS PROCESS.

THIRD, THE ORGANIZATIONS UPON WHICH THE GOVERNMENT CONFERS THE RIGHT TO RECEIVE THE PROCEEDS OF COIN SALES ARE SUBJECT TO LITTLE, IF ANY, GOVERNMENT OVERSIGHT. THE WASHINGTON TIMES RECENTLY REPORTED THAT THE BATTLE OF NORMANDY FOUNDATION, WHICH HAS RECEIVED

3 MILLION DOLLARS FROM A COIN TO BUILD A MEMORIAL AT NORMANDY, HAS SPENT 90% OF ITS MONEY ON TRAVEL, ENTERTAINMENT, FUNDRAISING, AND THE PERSONAL EXPENSES OF ITS PRESIDENT, A MAN NAMED TONY STOUT. TO MY KNOWLEDGE, THE MEMORIAL IS YET TO BE BUILT -- AND MAY NEVER BE BUILT.

FOURTH, AND FINALLY, THE PROLIFERATION OF COINS ON THE MARKET IS HAVING A NEGATIVE IMPACT ON THE SALES OF EACH COIN. ALTHOUGH EACH COIN PROGRAM MAY HAVE ITS OWN UNIQUE CONSTITUENCY, THE MINT TELLS US THAT BY AND LARGE THE BULK OF THE MARKET CONSISTS OF 2 MILLION OR SO DEVOTED COIN COLLECTORS. IN FACT, THE MINT TELLS US THAT 90% OF THE COINS SOLD IN A TYPICAL PROGRAM GO TO THESE SAME COLLECTORS. OVER THE LAST 7 YEARS, THERE HAVE BEEN 12 COMMEMORATIVE COINS PUT ONTO THE MARKET. ON AVERAGE, THESE COINS ARE SELLING LESS AND LESS, BECAUSE SUPPLY IS OUTPACING DEMAND.

IT IS CLEAR TO ME THAT WE NEED TO REFORM THE WAY WE GO ABOUT ENACTING AND OVERSEEING COMMEMORATIVE COIN PROGRAMS. WE DON'T WANT TO KILL THE GOOSE THAT LAYS THE GOLDEN EGGS BY SATURATING THE MARKET, AND DRIVING PRICES SO LOW THAT NO ORGANIZATION CAN MEET ITS GOALS.

ACCORDINGLY, IT IS MY INTENTION TO PURSUE -- WITH MR. MCCANDLESS, OTHER MEMBERS OF THE COMMITTEE, AND THE MINT -- SEVERAL CHANGES IN THE MINTING PROCESS. I WOULD SUGGEST THAT WE CONSIDER THE FOLLOWING STEPS:

* ONE, A CAP ON THE NUMBER OF COINS THAT CAN BE ENACTED IN ANY ONE YEAR, TO BE DETERMINED ON THE ADVICE OF THE COIN COMMISSION ESTABLISHED LAST CONGRESS;

* TWO, GAO AUDITS OF FOUNDATIONS THAT RECEIVE AND SPEND THE

PROCEEDS OF COIN SALES, ALONG WITH QUARTERLY FINANCIAL REPORTING TO THE MINT, IN ORDER TO PREVENT WASTE AND ABUSE;

* THREE, REQUIRING THESE FOUNDATIONS TO SHARE IN SOME OF THE UP-FRONT COSTS OF MINTING, IN ORDER TO PROVE THEIR SERIOUSNESS;

* AND FOUR, ENSURING THAT ANY WINDFALLS IN THE SALE OF COINS BE SHARED BY THE TREASURY, AND NOT HORDED BY A GIVEN COIN FOUNDATION. LET'S NOT FORGET THAT IT'S ONLY BECAUSE OF THE GOVERNMENT'S UNIQUE POWER TO MINT THAT FOUNDATIONS CAN RAISE MILLIONS OF DOLLARS; I DON'T THINK IT'S TOO MUCH TO ASK THAT THE TAXPAYERS WHO SUPPORT THE GOVERNMENT SHARE SOME OF THE BENEFITS.

I WANT TO THANK ALL OF OUR WITNESSES FOR APPEARING THIS AFTERNOON, PARTICULARLY CONGRESSMEN BONIOR, RIDGE, PETERSON, AND PAYNE. I ALSO WANT TO THANK MR. ESSNER FROM THE MINT, AND OUR OTHER WITNESSES FOR TAKING THE TIME TO FIT INTO THE CONGRESS' BUSY SCHEDULE. WE VERY MUCH APPRECIATE YOUR COOPERATION.

WITH THAT, LET ME TURN THE MICROPHONE OVER TO MR. MCCANDLESS, AND THANK HIM FOR AGREEING TO HAVE TODAY'S HEARING WITH AN ABBREVIATED NOTICE.

**Testimony by David E. Bonior**
**to the Subcommittee on Consumer Credit and Insurance**

11/10/93
on

## H.R. 1608

---

I would like to thank the Chairman for holding these hearings. My statement will be brief.

When I first came to Congress in 1977, I joined with several of my colleagues in founding the Vietnam-Era Veterans in Congress.

We believed that we must heal the wounds of the Vietnam war, bring torn generations together and raise the consciousness of the American people so a war like that would never be fought again.

There was just a handful of us, but we were determined to get health and retirement benefits for Vietnam vets, help for victims of Agent Orange and for victims of post traumatic stress syndrome, and, above all, bring some sense of dignity to those who came back from an unpopular war.

We knew we were fighting an uphill battle when we suggested that we needed a memorial in the nation's capital for the Vietnam war. We did not have much political support to start with, but through the volunteer efforts of numerous Vietnam vets we got it done. Today, the Vietnam Veterans Memorial, built and maintained by private donations, is the most visited memorial in the country. Every person who visits the Wall, young or old, leaves with an impression about what that time must have been like. It gives them an awareness that history books can never teach.

Most importantly, the Wall was built to heal. To heal the pain and suffering, to heal the emotional scars and wounds, to heal the spirits and souls of those who rushed to forget not only the war, but those who fought in Vietnam.

One needs only to see the family tracing the name of a loved one, the woman weeping while kneeling to place a wreath at the base of the Wall, the proud man wearing his fatigues as he stares at the names of his buddies and wonders why, to know the healing power of the Wall.

Mr. Chairman, I had the honor of participating in the Memorial Day services at the Wall this year. I heard nurse Janis Nark struggle to hold back the tears as she told of how the Memorial helped her heal. I heard all-pro football player Derek Thomas, who did not want to leave the podium on his first visit, talk proudly of his father whose name is on the Wall. Through the years we have seen the Memorial help do what we set out to do --- help to heal the wounds of an unpopular war.

Now the Wall needs our help. A June 1990 report identified the following problems:

1. Cracks on 19 of the panels.
2. Chips on panels 72E, 69E, 20E and 49W.
3. Many other panels nicked and permanently scratched.
4. Many other panels showing signs of differential settlement.

In 1991, the cost of replacing the granite panels was projected to be upwards of $2 million.

In 1992, the Vietnam Veterans Memorial Fund replaced the granite walkways and reset the lights at the site --- a project that cost $200,000.

These are just a few examples, and I will let others who will be testifying later elaborate on the needs of the Wall.

Mr. Chairman, the Vietnam Veterans Memorial Coin Act will provide a permanent maintenance endowment for the Memorial. The bill will direct the Secretary of the Treasury to mint 500,000 coins. With a surcharge of 10 dollars we will help raise approximately five million dollars to ensure that the Wall will be standing for generations to come.

More importantly, the coin itself will help in the healing process. While many coin collectors will purchase the coin, the market is much larger. Think of the Vietnam veterans, their friends and families who will buy these coins to support the Wall and help them ensure that their children and grandchildren never forget the Vietnam war.

The remarkable men and women who served our country can teach us all about bravery, sacrifice and courage. We must make sure that our children and our nation always remember them . . . because, in the end, that is the highest tribute we can pay.

And that is why, Mr. Chairman, 316 of my colleagues and myself, believe your Subcommittee should favorably report H.R. 1608 to the full Banking Committee and we should pass this bill before we adjourn this first session of Congress.

TESTIMONY OF
REP. L.F. PAYNE, M.C.
HOUSE BANKING COMMITTEE
SUBCOMMITTEE ON CONSUMER CREDIT AND INSURANCE
H.R. 789

MR. CHAIRMAN AND MEMBERS OF THE SUBCOMMITTEE.

THANK YOU FOR HOLDING THIS HEARING TODAY, AND FOR TAKING UP MY BILL, H.R. 789, TO AUTHORIZE THE MINTING OF A COIN COMMEMORATING THE 250TH ANNIVERSARY OF THOMAS JEFFERSON'S BIRTH.

I ALSO WANT TO EXPRESS MY PARTICULAR THANKS TO THOSE OF YOU WHO ARE CO-SPONSORS OF THIS BILL, TOTALLING ALMOST ONE-HALF OF THE MEMBERSHIP OF THIS SUBCOMMITTEE. THIS IS A BI-PARTISAN BILL, IT IS SUPPORTED BY ALL THE MEMBERS OF THE VIRGINIA DELEGATION, IT CURRENTLY HAS 253 COSPONSORS IN THE HOUSE AND IS ONE OF ONLY TWO COIN BILLS THAT HAS ALREADY PASSED THE SENATE.

MR. CHAIRMAN, THIS IS AN IMPORTANT YEAR IN THE HISTORY OF THOMAS JEFFERSON. PRESIDENT CLINTON BEGAN HIS INAUGURAL CELEBRATION AT MONTICELLO, IN HONOR OF THOMAS JEFFERSON, THE ARCHITECT OF OUR DEMOCRATIC SYSTEM OF GOVERNMENT. THROUGHOUT THE YEAR, HALLMARK DATES IN THOMAS JEFFERSON'S LIFE HAVE BEEN HONORED BY SPECIAL COMMEMORATIVE EVENTS AND CELEBRATIONS, NOT ONLY AT PROPERTIES SUCH AS POPLAR FOREST AND MONTICELLO, BUT THROUGHOUT THE COUNTRY.

THE SPIRIT OF CELEBRATION HAS EXTENDED BEYOND OUR BORDERS WITH COUNTRIES THROUGHOUT THE WORLD JOINING TOGETHER TO HONOR THIS GREAT AMERICAN PATRIOT. MONTICELLO'S CELEBRATION INCLUDED A VISIT BY FORMER PRESIDENT OF THE SOVIET UNION MICHAEL GORBACHEV.

IT IS BECAUSE OF THE INTERNATIONAL SCOPE OF THIS YEAR'S CELEBRATION THAT I INITIALLY INTRODUCED H.R. 789, AND WHY I HAVE ARGUED FOR ITS PASSAGE THIS YEAR SO PASSIONATELY. I FIRMLY BELIEVE THAT THIS COIN WILL REACH A CONSTITUENCY THAT EXTENDS WELL BEYOND THE USUAL COMMUNITY OF COIN COLLECTORS. MONTICELLO ALONE EXPECTS CLOSE TO ONE QUARTER OF A MILLION PEOPLE TO TOUR JEFFERSON'S HOME DURING THE REMAINING MONTHS OF THIS YEAR. I FIRMLY BELIEVE THAT MANY OF THESE VISITORS WOULD APPRECIATE THE OPPORTUNITY TO FURTHER HONOR JEFFERSON BY PURCHASING A COIN IN HIS HONOR.

MR. CHAIRMAN, H.R. 789 WAS DRAFTED WITH CAREFUL CONSIDERATION FOR THE CONCERNS THIS SUBCOMMITTEE HAS EXPRESSED IN THE PAST ABOUT COIN BILLS. IT AUTHORIZES A VERY SMALL NUMBER OF COINS TO BE ISSUED, ONLY 600,000, AND THE ONE-DOLLAR DENOMINATION WAS SELECTED TO MAKE THE COIN AFFORDABLE TO THE GENERAL PUBLIC. THE ONLY OTHER COIN AUTHORIZED UNDER SUCH LIMITATIONS, THE WHITE HOUSE COIN BILL, SOLD OUT ITS ENTIRE ISSUE IN 10 DAYS. WE BELIEVE THIS COIN WILL DO AT LEAST AS WELL.

THE PROJECTS THAT WILL BE SUPPORTED BY THE PROCEEDS FROM THE SALE OF THE COINS ARE WELL KNOWN BY JEFFERSONIAN SCHOLARS AND BY THE GENERAL PUBLIC. IN THE CASE OF MONTICELLO, THE PROCEEDS FROM H.R. 789 WILL FUND MONTICELLO'S FIRST GENERAL ENDOWMENT AND ADVANCE ITS PRIMARY MISSION OF EDUCATION AND PRESERVATION.

MONTICELLO IS THE ONLY AMERICAN HOME EVER NAMED TO UNESCO'S WORLD HERITAGE LIST, ALONG WITH SUCH INTERNATIONAL TREASURES AS THE TAJ MAHAL, THE PYRAMIDS OF EGYPT, VERSAILLES AND THE GREAT WALL OF CHINA. THIS PRICELESS PIECE OF OUR HERITAGE RECENTLY HAD ITS ROOF REDONE. FOR THE FIRST TIME IN DECADES THE CEILINGS AREN'T DRIPPING, THE WALLS AREN'T DAMP AND MOLD ISN'T FLOURISHING IN ITS RAFTERS, BUT MUCH ELSE REMAINS TO BE DONE. THE ENDOWMENT ESTABLISHED WITH THE PROCEEDS FROM THE COIN SALE WILL ASSIST IN THIS EFFORT.

IN ORDER TO RECREATE THE APPEARANCE OF THE HOME DURING JEFFERSON'S TIME, THE FOUNDATION SPENT FOUR YEARS GATHERING PERSONAL POSSESSIONS FROM AS FAR AWAY AS PARIS, FRANCE, AND PERSUADING THEIR CURRENT OWNERS TO LEND THEM FOR A YEAR-LONG EXHIBITION. LITTLE MONEY EXISTS TO PURCHASE THESE TREASURES AND RETURN THEM TO THEIR RIGHTFUL HOME. THIS IS ANOTHER AREA WHICH WILL BE SUPPORTED BY THE ENDOWMENT.

PROCEEDS FROM THE COIN SALE WILL ALSO BE USED FOR POPLAR FOREST, THOMAS JEFFERSON'S PERSONAL RETREAT. THE FOUNDATION ATTEMPTING TO SAVE POPLAR FOREST FOR FUTURE GENERATIONS FACES AN EVEN MORE DAUNTING TASK. POPLAR FOREST, THE FIRST OCTAGONAL HOUSE BUILT IN VIRGINIA WAS STRUCK TWICE BY FIRE AND UNDERWENT "RENOVATIONS" THAT CHANGED ITS STYLE AND APPEARANCE. PAINSTAKING RESEARCH WAS REQUIRED TO ESTABLISH EXACTLY WHAT THE HOUSE LOOKED LIKE IN JEFFERSON'S TIME.

NOW SUPPORTERS ARE IN A RACE AGAINST TIME TO PROCEED WITH RESTORATION BEFORE THE BUILDING SUFFERS IRREPARABLE STRUCTURAL DAMAGE. A $6.6 MILLION DOLLAR RESTORATION CAMPAIGN WAS LAUNCHED IN THE SPRING. ALTHOUGH $2.1 MILLION HAS ALREADY BEEN RAISED FROM CONTRIBUTORS, LARGE AND SMALL, THROUGHOUT THE COUNTRY, THIS IS FAR SHORT OF THE GOAL. PROJECTS INCLUDED IN PHASE ONE BECAUSE OF THEIR HIGH PRIORITY AND CRITICAL NATURE INCLUDE THE REBUILDING OF THE SOUTH PORTICO, RESTORATION OF THE FOUNDATION AND DRAINAGE IMPROVEMENT.

MR. CHAIRMAN, I HAVE A PICTURE HERE THAT I WOULD LIKE TO SHARE WITH THE SUBCOMMITTEE THAT SHOWS THE CURRENT CONDITION OF POPLAR FOREST. AS YOU CAN SEE, TIME IS OF THE ESSENCE FOR THIS PROJECT. IN ADDITION, MR. CHAIRMAN, I WOULD LIKE TO ASK UNANIMOUS CONSENT THAT A STATEMENT FROM THE CORPORATION FOR JEFFERSON'S POPLAR FOREST BE INCLUDED IN THE RECORD OF THIS HEARING.

MR. CHAIRMAN, WHEN THIS NATION COMMEMORATED THE 200TH ANNIVERSARY OF THOMAS JEFFERSON'S BIRTH, CONGRESS PASSED LEGISLATION AUTHORIZING THE CONSTRUCTION OF THE JEFFERSON MEMORIAL ON THE MALL. I BELIEVE AUTHORIZING THE MINTING OF A COMMEMORATIVE COIN IN HIS HONOR IS THE LEAST WE CAN DO TO HONOR THE 250TH ANNIVERSARY.

I STRONGLY URGE THIS COMMITTEE TO APPROVE H.R. 789 AND TO SUPPORT PASSAGE BY THE HOUSE BEFORE WE ADJOURN THIS LEGISLATIVE SESSION.

THANK YOU.

THOMAS JEFFERSON'S POPLAR FOREST: BEFORE RESTORATION

Front of main house (above), Rear of main house (below)

## THOMAS JEFFERSON'S POPLAR FOREST
## and the
## JEFFERSON COMMEMORATIVE COIN ACT

In 1993, the nation has been celebrating the 250th anniversary of Thomas Jefferson's birth. One fitting way for the Government of the United States to observe this occasion is to help its citizens ensure the survival of Poplar Forest for future generations of Americans, as Mt. Vernon and Monticello were rescued for us.

Poplar Forest, located in Bedford County, Virginia, is one of only two homes designed and built by Jefferson for his own use. An avid classicist, he lavished his mature architectural talent on the design and building of his personal retreat which the Secretary of the Interior has designated a National Historic Landmark. Assessing his own design, Jefferson said of Poplar Forest, "When finished, it will be the best dwelling house in the state, except that of Monticello; perhaps preferable to that, as more proportioned to the faculties of a private citizen."

It is extraordinary to realize that the home of a founding father, a place so important to Thomas Jefferson, came so close to being lost. Privately owned since Jefferson created it, Poplar Forest became endangered in 1983. A small group of private citizens launched a grass-roots effort to save it for the cultural and educational benefit of the public. Contributions from more than 2,100 donors, including school children and people from all walks of life, have made it possible to buy the threatened landmark.

The non-profit Corporation for Jefferson's Poplar Forest opened the property so that people could have access to this landmark for the first time. People from all 50 states and from 30 foreign countries have come to see Poplar Forest in its present condition, and to watch the preeminent restoration team of architects and archaeologists carefully identifying the original features of Jefferson's buildings and landscape, and starting the bricks-and-mortar restoration of the main house.

Restoring such a significant property is an undertaking of great responsibility. We ask the Government of the United States to help us preserve Jefferson's legacy at Poplar Forest. Over $9 million has been raised for the property acquisition and restoration since the rescue began. Passage of the Commemorative Coin legislation would assist in carrying forward the bricks-and-mortar restoration of Jefferson's octagonal house and the archaeological investigation of the grounds, help in further developing the landmark for increased public access for educational use, aide in purchasing the additional land at the heart of the plantation necessary for protection of the historic viewshed, and could also help provide for the creation of an endowment for this national landmark.

At Poplar Forest, citizens of America and of the world can be reminded of Jefferson and his legacies to society. In addition, Poplar Forest can provide insight into his ideas about the ideal life of a private citizen because he designed his retreat as an embodiment of those ideas. Gaining that insight is as relevant to us as individuals as Jefferson's ideas about government are relevant to our society.

If we are accountable to those who succeed us, we have today an exceptional opportunity to demonstrate that trust. Once in a great while we have the opportunity to achieve something significant, something that will endure. The protection, restoration, and preservation of Thomas Jefferson's Poplar Forest for future generations is such an opportunity.

The Corporation for Jefferson's Poplar Forest
November 1993

## TESTIMONY OF THE HONORABLE TOM RIDGE

## SUBCOMMITTEE ON CONSUMER CREDIT AND INSURANCE
## COMMITTEE ON BANKING

**November 10, 1993**

**Mr. Chairman, thank you for scheduling today's hearing. I am honored to appear before you today with my colleague, David Bonior, and Jan Scruggs, the Director of the Vietnam Veterans Memorial Fund. I would like to strongly urge this Subcommittee to pass H.R. 1608, the "1994 Vietnam Veterans Memorial Commemorative Coin Act."**

**It is appropriate that a hearing to consider H.R. 1608 be held on the eve of the day set aside to honor those that have served this country. Veterans' Day is only one of the many ways that America demonstrates the debt of gratitude owed to those who protect its principles.**

**The legislation that David Bonior and I have introduced would require that the Secretary of the Treasury mint coins to commemorate the 10th anniversary of the Vietnam Veterans Memorial. This is a bipartisan bill, cosponsored by over 300 of our colleagues, including a majority from the**

**Banking Committee. I strongly believe that the Vietnam Veterans Memorial, commonly known as the Wall, is deserving of such commemoration.**

**Vietnam was the longest war in the history of our nation, lasting from July of 1957 to May of 1975. Each of the 2.5 million men and women who served the military in Vietnam endured a unique experience and each remembers in an individual and personal way that experience 20 years later -- myself included.**

**The Wall welds these experiences together to remind all Americans of what can be lost when a country goes to war. It is a representative grave for the 58,000 men and women that died in service to their country and a reminder to all Americans that there are still 2,266 persons listed as Missing in Action.**

**A coin commemorating the Vietnam Veterans Memorial will once again recognize these brave soldiers and the ultimate sacrifice they have made for their country. This legislation will also be an opportunity for the United States Government to pay special tribute to those that wore the**

country's uniform during the Vietnam-era. This recognition of Vietnam veterans is not only deserving, but appropriate.

I know that legislation has already been passed to authorize a coin program for the World Cup in 1994. And that there is concern that passing legislation to mint coins to commemorate the Vietnam Memorial in 1994 will flood the numismatic community and jeopardize both of these laudable coin programs. However, the market for the Vietnam Memorial Commemorative coin will reach far beyond those that would ordinarily participate in coin collection.

The Wall is the most visited memorial in the United States, drawing more than 2.5 million visitors annually. These visitors do not leave without being personally and emotionally affected -- be it because they are remembering the loss of a loved one, remembering their own experiences in Vietnam and friends that did not return, or because the Memorial is a stark reminder to the cruelty of war. Mr. Chairman, these are the people that will purchase this coin.

It is appropriate that we authorize the Secretary of the Treasury to

**mint these coins in 1994 because it will be the 10th anniversary of the addition of Frederick E. Hart's seven-foot bronze statue, The Three Servicemen, and a flagpole to the Memorial. It will also be 10 years since the Vietnam Veterans Memorial Fund (VVMF) gave the Memorial to the U.S. government. The VVMF did retain certain rights and responsibilities under a memorandum of conveyance signed by President Reagan.**

**Through issuing 500,000 coins, the legislation will raise approximately five million dollars to permanently endow the Memorial. The bill is revenue neutral, and will ultimately represent a savings to the government as it precludes the need for any future appropriation to repair the Wall.**

**Once again, I thank this Subcommittee for the opportunity to testify on behalf of H.R. 1608 and ask that you report it to the full Committee as expeditiously as possible.**

TESTIMONY

Before
THE SUBCOMMITTEE ON CONSUMER CREDIT AND INSURANCE
November 10, 1993

By
CONGRESSMAN PETE PETERSON
2nd District, Florida

Mr. Chairman, thank you for the opportunity to testify before your Subcommittee.

I would like to begin by telling the Subcommittee a little bit about the Andersonville National Historic Site, which is the only park in the National Park System to serve as a memorial to all Americans ever held as prisoners of war. Andersonville, or Camp Sumter as it was officially known, was the largest of many Confederate military prisons established during the Civil War. During the time that Andersonville existed, more than 45,000 Union soldiers were confined here. Of these, almost 13,000 died from disease, poor sanitation, malnutrition, overcrowding, or exposure to the elements.

The total number of American Prisoners of War held from World War I, World War II, the Korean War, and the Vietnam War is 142,206. This number does not include the number of Americans held prisoners during our most recent wars, such as the Gulf War and our involvement in Somalia, but this number does give all of us an idea of the number of Americans who have suffered and endured as POWs. As of January 1, 1993, the number of POWs still living is 66,767.

With the history of POWs being as old as the history of warfare, it is extremely unfortunate that our nation has not adequately acknowledged the sacrifices of our POWs in any permanent symbolic manner. My bill, The Prisoner of War Commemorative Coin Act, H.R. 535, will help correct that oversight by recognizing the sacrifices of those Americans who lost their lives as POWs plus honor those still living.

While the proposed coin will serve as the physical symbol of the Nation's gratitude to our POWs; it will also serve as a funding vehicle to help complete construction on the already authorized Andersonville POW Museum, located at the Andersonville National Historic Site in Georgia. A portion of the proceeds will also help defray the cost of maintaining our national cemeteries.

After recovering the cost of minting the coins, the first $3 million in receipts from the sales of these coins will help complete construction of the Museum. The next $1 million will go into an endowment fund, which will pay for the maintenance of the Museum. All remaining amounts shall be paid to the Secretary of Veterans Affairs for the purpose of maintaining our national cemeteries.

The Senate Committee on Finance passed identical legislation (S. 483) earlier this year. By allowing Congress to take up this legislation, we will begin the healing process by giving permanent recognition to our POWs and the families who have made great, and for some, the ultimate sacrifice for their country.

This bill has strong bipartisan support as well as the public support of the American Ex-Prisoners of War, Defenders of Bataan and Corrigidor, Korean Ex-Prisoners of War, NAM-POWS, League of Families, and other individual unit organizations.

Mr. Chairman, I appreciate the opportunity to testify before your Subcommittee on this very important legislation. I will be happy to answer any questions.

# Statement of

# Honorable G. V. (Sonny) Montgomery

# on H. R. 1697

# before the

# Subcommittee on Consumer Credit and Insurance

# November 10, 1993

Mr. Chairman, I appreciate the opportunity to express my views on H.R. 1697, the "Women in Military Service for America Memorial Commemorative Coin Act." The bill, which has more than 260 cosponsors, would direct the Secretary of the Treasury to issue five-dollar gold coins and one-dollar silver coins symbolic of women's service in the Armed Forces. The sale of these coins will be crucial in the effort to raise funds to build this long overdue memorial.

The Women in Military Service for America Memorial, which will be constructed at the main gate of Arlington National Cemetery, will recognize the patriotism and courage of the 1.8 million women who have served our country in Somalia, the Persian Gulf, Vietnam, Korea, World Wars II and I, and U.S. conflicts dating back to the American Revolution, as well as those who have served in peacetime.

The Congress authorized the memorial in 1986 in Public Law 99-610. The Women In Military Service For America Memorial Foundation was designated as administrator of this project. Since that time, the Foundation has been working to educate the public about the role of women in the military and has taken actions necessary to construct the memorial. The federal approval agencies have all unanimously and enthusiastically approved the design concept. The proceeds from the sale of the coins will help assure funding to construct the memorial -- the remaining major task to be completed.

Both the Memorial and the coins will be tangible reminders to this and future generations of the contributions that women have made in defending and serving our country.

Women have served the cause of freedom under difficult and dangerous circumstances as nurses, saboteurs, scouts, couriers, switchboard operators, stenographers, translators, pilots and gunner's mates. A number have been highly decorated (including combat-related awards), some were prisoners of war, some remain buried in U.S. cemeteries overseas, and they all have been important to both wartime and peacetime efforts. We owe a great debt to women for their contributions to our national security and well-being.

Mr. Chairman, the women who have served in our Armed Forces have earned a special place of distinction in our history and our hearts. I urge favorable consideration of this coin legislation to ensure construction of the Memorial and to commemorate the proud tradition of service rendered by women in the military.

Finally, Mr. Chairman, I understand that the Treasury Department may propose that this and two other "veteran" coin bills -- one commemorating Americans who have been prisoners of war and another the 10th anniversary of the Vietnam Veterans Memorial -- be consolidated and that the proceeds from the sale of the coins be equally divided among the three specified beneficiary groups. In my view, women veterans and the individuals honored by the other coin bills would object to this, and rightfully so. Each is deserving of distinctive tribute. I hope you will reject this proposal and report the coin bills separately. To do otherwise would greatly diminish the worthy objectives of all three.

# # #

**STATEMENT OF EUGENE H. ESSNER, DEPUTY DIRECTOR**
**UNITED STATES MINT**
**BEFORE THE SUBCOMMITTEE ON CONSUMER CREDIT AND INSURANCE**
**HOUSE BANKING COMMITTEE**
**Wednesday, November 10, 1993**

Good Afternoon Mr. Chairman and members of the Subcommittee. Thank you for the opportunity to express the views of the Treasury Department concerning the following commemorative coin bills --

(1) H.R. 535, the "Prisoner-of-War Commemorative Coin Act";

(2) H.R. 789, the "Jefferson Commemorative Coin Act of 1993";

(3) H.R. 1608, the "1994 Vietnam Veterans Memorial Commemorative Coin Act"; and

(4) H.R. 1697, the "Women in Military Service for American Memorial Commemorative Coin Act".

H.R. 535 mandates the issuance of not more than 1.5 million silver coins for the period of January 15, 1994 through December 31, 1994 in honor of Americans who have been prisoners of war. The Jefferson bill, H.R. 789, commemorates the 250th anniversary of the birth of Thomas Jefferson with the minting of not more than 600,000 silver coins from July 4, 1993 through July 4, 1994. The Vietnam Veterans Memorial bill, H.R. 1608, requires the production of not more than 500,000 silver coins in commemoration of the 10th anniversary of the Memorial for the period of April

1, 1994 through April 1, 1995. Lastly, H.R. 1697 commemorates American women who have served in the military with the issuance of not more than 50,000 gold and 500,000 silver coins beginning on November 1, 1993 and ending on December 31, 1994.

As you know, on May 27, 1993, the Senate passed S. 50, the Senate companion bill to H.R. 789, the Jefferson bill, and on September 21, 1993, the Senate Banking Committee favorably reported out the companion bills of the three veteran bills under consideration here today.

The Department of the Treasury has been a consistent voice for limiting the growth of commemorative coin programs. We often find ourselves in the unenviable position of being torn between worthwhile and sympathetic causes and events for which a group is seeking commemoration, and the need to avoid saturating the commemorative coin market. This is another such occasion. The Department of the Treasury opposes these bills as currently drafted. This opposition is not because of any belief that the subject matter of the coins is inappropriate, but rather to protect the commemorative coin market as a whole. If Congress nonetheless chooses to authorize another commemorative coin bill for 1994, we believe the most viable option would be to consolidate the three bills that commemorate veterans groups. Properly structured, one coin program, with the proceeds divided among the sponsoring organizations, would increase chances of success for all sponsoring organizations.

While we have no objection to the merits of the Thomas Jefferson coin legislation, we are concerned over having at least three coin programs in 1994, and perhaps as many as five. We urge that it be submitted to the Citizens Commemorative Coin Advisory Committee for a recommendation on timing.

Since the early 1980s, Congress has authorized 18 commemorative coin programs. Two of the already authorized programs for 1994 - 1996 are among the largest programs ever undertaken by the Mint. The 1994 World Cup program authorizes the issuance of up to 10.75 million gold, silver, and clad coins. The 1995/1996 Olympic program, the most ambitious ever launched, requires the issuance of 16 coins (4 gold coins, 8 silver coins and 4 clad coins) during a two-year period for a total of up to 17.95 million coins. In addition, the Civil War coin program authorizes up to 3.3 million gold, silver and clad coins in 1995. To put these ambitious programs in a larger context, only one of the dozen commemorative coin programs of the past seven years has registered sales of 4 million coins. The veterans coin programs and the Jefferson program would be competing for marketing resources and limited collector disposable income with the already authorized programs, and with each other as well.

The enabling legislation for commemorative coin programs

generally mandates that a portion of the coin sale proceeds, usually designated as surcharges, is to be paid to a designated recipient organization. Over $300 million in surcharges have been generated from Mint commemorative coin sales since the 1984 Olympic coin program. Sales figures from the coin programs since 1986, however, reflect a declining interest in commemorative coins by the numismatic community, which constitutes about 90% of coin purchasers. The 1986 Statue of Liberty commemorative coin program raised approximately $83 million in surcharges; the 1992 Olympic program raised only $9 million. We believe that it is critical that the number of commemorative coin programs be limited in order to stem the falling demand for commemorative coins, foster an effective secondary market, and ensure the success of future coin programs.

Numerous coin programs offered during the same time period compete with each other. This competition threatens the success of the individual programs and is likely to result in below expectation sales for all of the programs. This was clearly apparent when the U.S.O. commemorative coin program, which was the third program for 1991, had very low sales relative to the first two programs of that year.

We fully recognize, however, that these concerns cannot easily reverse the current tide of commemorative coinage, especially when there are so many worthwhile causes supported by these programs. Congress has begun to address this problem with its enactment of legislation establishing the Citizens Commemorative Coin Advisory Committee. The key purpose of the Committee, which was created in response to concern over the growing proliferation of commemorative coin bills, is to provide advice to Congress on the selection of subjects for commemorative coins. For your information, we are in the final stages of setting up the Committee. After soliciting nominations for membership through the Federal Register and the media, receiving applications, and reviewing approximately 80 resumes and conducting interviews, we are ready to make final recommendations to the Secretary of the Treasury. The Committee should be fully operational before the end of the year, and we hope it will be instrumental in exacting greater control over the number of bills enacted.

In the interim, if legislation is to be enacted, the Mint proposes that the three veterans bills be converted from separate, competing programs to a consolidated commemorative coin program. A merger would allow all of the designated recipient organizations to benefit from the collection of surcharges from a three-coin series. We believe that one combined program would be more successful and more efficiently marketed and managed than multiple programs offered during the same time period.

We recommend that an omnibus veterans commemorative coin bill be drafted to provide the Mint maximum flexibility to structure a highly marketable coin program. We also recommend that the bill provide for low mintage levels and limited availability of the coins. Reduced mintage levels would increase total revenue for designated recipients. A combined program would also allow us to better dedicate resources to the project. To this end, we would be happy to work with the Subcommittee to develop alternative legislation.

If, however, the bills go forward as currently drafted, we have the following technical comments. The starting date proposed in the Jefferson bill was this past July, and we seriously question whether the Mint could effectively, if at all, produce and market this coin program by its completion date of July 1994. Moreover, it is simply not practical to set the starting dates for this month and January 1994 as proposed by H.R. 1697 and H.R. 535, respectively. It generally takes at least six months from passage of legislation to the beginning of coin production. Lead-time is required by the Mint to select designs, produce dies, conduct trial strikes, procure boxes, etc.

We also believe that the total number of silver coins offered in each commemorative coin program should be restricted to 500,000 coins. H.R. 535, the POW bill, calls for a mintage level of 1.5 million silver coins. This amount is simply too high to ensure collector interest. Setting the maximum mintage at a level slightly below sales projections generates greater interest in a coin program by developing a secondary market and actually increases demand for the coin and the surcharges that can be collected. For example, the 1992 White House Commemorative Coin program offered a silver coin program with a maximum mintage level of only 500,000 coins for a single year program. All coins sold out in less than three weeks, and the value of these coins have increased since the sell-out.

H.R. 535 also requires the funding mechanism for the program to be the Coinage Profit Fund which is no longer in use for commemorative coin programs. The Numismatic Public Enterprise Fund is the proper funding source. Lastly, two of the veteran bills (H.R. 535 and H.R. 1697) call for the coins to bear a "1993" date, rather than "1994", the year the coins will be issued. Experience shows that coin collectors prefer commemorative coins which are offered inscribed with the current year's date. The Jefferson bill, H.R. 789, also mandates a "1993" dated coin since 1993 is the 250th anniversary year of the birth of Jefferson. While we realize the significance of using "1993", the same numismatic concerns would apply.

Thank you again for convening this hearing and for giving us the opportunity to share with the Subcommittee the Treasury Department's views on these bills, specifically, and on commemorative coinage, generally.

## WOMEN ON COINS OF THE UNITED STATES

*Actual Individuals:*

Queen Isabella of Spain
  1893 Columbian Exposition Commemorative Quarter Dollar
Ellinor Dare and Virginia Dare
  1937 Roanoke Island, North Carolina Commemorative Half Dollar
Susan B. Anthony
  1979-1981 Regular Issue Dollar

*Female Representations:*

Colonial*
  1987 Constitution Bicentennial Commemorative Silver Dollar
Gymnast
  1992 XXV Olympiad Commemorative Clad Half Dollar
Immigrant*
  1986 Statue of Liberty Commemorative Half Dollar
Military*
  1993 World War II 50th Anniversary Commemorative Clad Half Dollar
Native American
  Regular Issue Cent, 1859-1909
Pioneer*
  1936 Elgin, Illinois Centennial Commemorative Half Dollar
Runner*
  1984 XXIII Olympiad Commemorative $10 Gold Eagle
Women's Industry
  1893 Columbian Exposition Commemorative Quarter Dollar

* *Part of a group*

All other representations have been allegorical in nature, and include: Liberty, Minerva, Justice, Peace, Victory, Columbia, and Freedom.

THE WOMEN IN MILITARY SERVICE FOR AMERICA MEMORIAL FOUNDATION, INC.

Dept. 560
Washington, DC 20042-0560

THE WOMEN'S MEMORIAL

(703) 533-1155
(800) 222-2294
(703) 931-4208 (FAX)

*Foundation Honorary Chair*
Hillary Rodham Clinton

*President*
Wilma L. Vaught
Brigadier General, USAF (Ret.)

*Campaign Honorary Chair*
Barbara P. Bush

November 10, 1993

**STATEMENT**

**H.R. 1697 Hearing**
**Consumer Credit and Insurance Subcommittee**

**Wilma L. Vaught, Brigadier General, USAF, Retired**
**President, Board of Directors**
**Women In Military Service For America Memorial Foundation, Inc.**

Mr. Chairman, Committee Members, speaking on behalf of the Board of Directors of the Women In Military Service Memorial Foundation, and representing the approximately 1.8 million military servicewomen, past and present, we respectfully request your approval of H.R. 1697 for gold and silver Commemorative Coins to be sold in 1994 with the surcharge to go to building the Women In Military Service For America Memorial.

The Women in Military Service Memorial, to be built at the gateway to Arlington National Cemetery, has an important story to tell. Through its "Register," exhibits and programs (like the Commemorative Coins), it will tell the story of more than two centuries of women's service, sacrifice and dedication in the defense of our nation -- a story that encompasses nearly two million women and the many more lives they have touched.

The history of women's roles in the American armed forces is an important piece of the fabric of this nation's history. It includes the story of:

- Deborah Sampson Gannett, who disguised herself as a man to fight in the Revolutionary War. She treated her own wounds to avoid detection;

- Clara Maass, a 26-year-old nurse who volunteered during the Spanish American War to help test Dr. Walter Reed's theory that a mosquito caused the spread of yellow fever. She died, but her death led to a cure;

- Seventy-seven women who were held prisoners of war by the Japanese during World War II, caring for the sick and wounded among hundreds of POWs in the Pacific theater, for nearly three years;

- Nurses serving in mobile units and hospitals on or near the front lines in World War I, World War II, Korea and Vietnam to save hundreds of thousands of lives.

In fact, women have served with valor and distinction throughout every major conflict and in times of peace in a variety of roles. It wasn't until Operation Desert Storm that we began to refer to our troops as the men and women of Desert Storm. Each of these women -- 1.8 million -- are veterans of the American armed forces, yet many have never considered themselves veterans or sought the benefits to which our veterans are entitled. This is partly due to the lack of recognition servicewomen have received throughout history. It is time to right that wrong.

It is important to note that, throughout the history of the commemorative coin program, only three have depicted specific female historical figures: the 1893 Commemorative Silver Dollar depicting Queen Isabella of Spain; the 350th Anniversary of Sir Walter Raleigh's lost Colony, depicting Ellinor Dare and her baby, released in 1937; and the Susan B. Anthony coin released in 1979 and 1981.

The Women In Military Service For America Memorial Foundation, Inc. (WIMSA) has received the necessary approvals for site and design concept and developed the fundraising initiatives necessary to bring us within sight of our goal of a 1994 groundbreaking. Passage of this coin bill is the last remaining hurdle. And, unlike other projects up for consideration, the timing for this bill is critical to the ultimate goal of building the national Memorial to the women who serve. WIMSA is prepared to work with Congress, the Consumer Credit Subcommittee and the U.S. Mint to ensure a successful marketing strategy for these commemorative coins. We fully understand the importance of not flooding the market with a plethora of coins. To do so, would ensure that none of the mintages would be successful. For that reason, we have been working with the U.S. Mint since first considering this bill to develop a sound marketing strategy. That strategy includes requesting a mintage that both the Mint and we feel will be successful as well as meet the needs of the Foundation.

We are proud to have the support of First Lady Hillary Rodham Clinton, Former First Lady Barbara P. Bush, all former living Presidents and Secretaries of Defense, more than 260 Members of Congress, the Department of Defense, the Military Coalition (representing 3.5 million members of the seven uniformed services), a majority of veteran organizations, including the American Legion and VFW, many of the nation's largest women's' organizations, foreign governments (Kuwait, Saudi Arabia and Qatar in honor of the women of Desert Storm) and state governments (five states have donated funds to honor their women veterans).

The Women's Memorial has garnered such unprecedented support for several reasons:

- It is the only national Memorial to recognize the service of all the women in every branch of service and in every major military conflict, as well as in times of peace.
- The only Memorial which uses an existing site, the historic gateway to Arlington National Cemetery (rather than displacing additional park lands). We are restoring and renovating the sadly neglected existing structures and incorporating them in a fitting and appropriate way into the design of the Memorial.

- The design was described by The Washington Post's architectural critic as "...the subtlest and most beautiful of the memorials proposed for the monumental core."

- It will provide a comprehensive record of the service and accomplishments of individual servicewomen through the computerized data base already being built.

Fundraising initiatives currently underway ensure that two-thirds of the needed funds will be available in 1994. Passage of the coin bill will provide the additional funding needed to break ground by the end of 1994. Work is in progress already for a geotechnical survey of the site and the schematic design, the first phase of detailed design development. Women veterans and active duty servicewomen across the country have worked tirelessly with us since 1986 to help make this happen. Their dreams can finally become reality -- and in the lifetime of some WW I women along with those who answered the call in WW II and Korea.

We urge you to support H.R. 1697 -- to send the message across the country that women's roles in the building and protecting of this nation from the American Revolution through Desert Storm will no longer be unrecognized and undervalued. Such recognition, so far lacking in this country's documentation of our history, will enrich not only America's servicewomen and women veterans, but every woman in every nation who will share in the pride and heritage of the achievements of those who paved the way.

## TESTIMONY OF JAN C. SCRUGGS

## PRESIDENT, VIETNAM VETERANS MEMORIAL FUND, INC.

## BEFORE THE

## HOUSE BANKING SUBCOMMITTEE

## ON CONSUMER CREDIT AND INSURANCE

## NOVEMBER 10, 1993

My name is Jan C. Scruggs. I am President of the Vietnam Veterans Memorial Fund ("VVMF"). I am appearing this afternoon, along with two members of the Memorial Fund's Board of Directors--Harry Robinson and Robert Frank--to testify in support of H.R. 1608. This legislation would authorize the minting of a Commemorative Coin recognizing the nation's most visited Memorial, the Vietnam Veterans Memorial.

Congress authorized the VVMF to build the Memorial on July 1, 1979. In November 1982, the Memorial was dedicated. In 1984, the Three Servicemen Statue was added along with the flagpole. All of these elements were built by the VVMF through private contributions made by the American People. Tomorrow yet another addition will be dedicated, the statue representing the women who served in Vietnam.

In 1984, VVMF gave the Memorial to the United States government. A Memorandum of Conveyance provided that VVMF would continue significant stewardship duties. These duties include:

1) hosting semi-annual ceremonies at the Memorial;
2) providing funds for repair and restoration of the Memorial;
3) providing funds in case of catastrophic damage to the Memorial and its various elements.

As part of this stewardship, VVMF has purchased eight granite panels and stored them at a secure location on the Quantico Marine Base. If funding becomes available, the VVMF would like to purchase enough granite so as to allow complete replacement of the Memorial's walls if this should ever be required. The granite would be cut, polished and put into place on outdoor frames where each panel would age and weather like the Memorial's walls. Although this might seem like an extraordinary precaution, we believe that it is warranted under circumstances I will explain.

This unique Memorial has difficulties which are in turn unique. Several of the Memorial's granite panels have developed cracks. These cracks may simply be attributable to flaws in the granite and may be unlikely to worsen; or, more ominously, they may be caused by the controversial system of pins and anchors on a concrete wall behind the granite panels, a support system which may be placing destructive stress on all the panels. Nationally recognized experts have studied the matter, and have provided us with contradictory conclusions. As a general matter, we have been advised to wait and see how much the cracking worsens. If it turns out that the panel support system is causing the cracking, the VVMF will face the extraordinary expense of disassembling the Memorial so that both the support system and the cracked panels can be replaced.

Apart from costs associated with the Memorial's walls, the extraordinary visitor traffic at the Memorial--many millions annually--creates significant repair requirements that need regular attention. For example, last year the VVMF spent some $200,000 repairing the Memorial's granite walkways and correcting certain lighting problems. These maintenance costs--which can be quite substantial--will continue for the foreseeable future.

What are the Memorial's needs? I have mentioned but a few. To provide an even more complete answer, we are currently laying the groundwork for an expert study, to be completed this summer, giving the VVMF an informed perspective about the projected problems over the next one hundred years. Repairs to the Wall, the statues, the walkways, the holders for the Directory of Names, and possible further walkways are examples of some of the projects necessary for future preservation of the Memorial.

Many have studied the Memorial to understand why it has such an extraordinary impact. Why are Americans drawn to this wall of polished granite? Why does this Wall of names cause people to leave emotionally charged items there? These and many other questions continue to attract informed speculation.

One thing is certain. The Vietnam Veterans Memorial is a national treasure and the VVMF is committed to maintaining and preserving the Memorial for future generations. Enactment of H.R. 1608 would assure the VVMF of the financial resources required to follow through on this commitment.

In closing, let me thank the Chair and the Committee for the opportunity to appear in support of H.R. 1608. We believe that Congress would be able to take great pride in the minting of a Commemorative Coin for the Vietnam Veterans Memorial, and that the revenues generated by such a coin could be put to no more deserving purpose than to assure the future of the nation's most visited Memorial.

Monticello
The Home of Thomas Jefferson
P.O. Box 316
Charlottesville, Virginia 22902

**STATEMENT OF DANIEL P. JORDAN, Ph.D.,**

**Executive Director,**

**The Thomas Jefferson Memorial Foundation (Monticello)**

**SUBMITTED TO THE**

**SUBCOMMITTEE ON CONSUMER CREDIT AND INSURANCE**

**The Honorable Joseph P. Kennedy II, Chairman,**

**Regarding H.R. 789:**

**"The Jefferson Commemorative Coin Act of 1993"**

**November 10, 1993**

Mr. Chairman, Members of the Subcommittee:

I speak with enthusiasm in support of H.R. 789 (The Jefferson Commemorative Coin Act of 1993) as introduced on February 3, 1993, by the Honorable L. F. Payne, Jr. (D-VA). The bill proposes the mintage of 600,000 one-dollar coins, 90 percent silver and 10 percent copper, as part of the commemoration in 1993 of the 250th anniversary of the birth of Thomas Jefferson. This commemoration provides a once-in-a-lifetime opportunity to recognize the man so eloquently quoted by advocates of freedom in Eastern Europe and in Tiananmen Square. The commemoration also represents an opportunity to inform all Americans of this nation's foremost apostle of democratic principles as well as perhaps this country's greatest

Renaissance man in his interests and contributions. The case for Mr. Jefferson is ably summarized by George Will who ranks Thomas Jefferson as no less than "the person of the millennium."

Mr. Chairman, we believe the case for H.R. 789 is compelling:

1) The Jefferson coin is timely. The 250th anniversary of Mr. Jefferson's birth is the appropriate occasion to mint a commemorative coin, which in turn will allow the American people to participate directly in the celebration.

2) The Jefferson coin has broad appeal. This project, from the beginning, has had the support of the United States Mint and is intended to celebrate Jefferson, the architect of democracy. Its appeal reaches far beyond the limited interests of professional coin collectors.

3) The Jefferson coin has overwhelming legislative support. The Senate approved S. 50 without opposition; 252 Representatives have signed to cosponsor H.R. 789; and the House leadership is in favor of it.

4) The Jefferson coin will not glut the market. The legislation is written for a limited number of coins, which the United States Mint believes will sell out quickly, as was the case with the White House commemorative coin that is the explicit model for H.R. 789.

5) The Jefferson coin will not cost the American taxpayer a penny. All expenses are covered in the coin's price to the public; a surcharge is added to benefit Jeffersonian causes and institutions (see pp. 4-5 in the bill).

6) The Jefferson coin will provide badly needed help for Monticello, which has been owned and operated since 1923 by the Thomas Jefferson Memorial Foundation, a private, nonprofit corporation.

Mr. Chairman, regarding this final point, I would like to elaborate on how the coin will help Monticello sustain the Jefferson legacy for the inspiration and edification of generations well into the 21st century and beyond.

As the home of Thomas Jefferson, Monticello will be visited by over 600,000 individuals during 1993. Twelve heads of state have come to Monticello in the last three years alone; and it was at Monticello this past January that the Clintons and Gores began their inaugural program and a new presidential administration. Monticello was ranked first in a recent national poll to determine "America's favorite buildings," and Monticello is the only home in America on the World Heritage List, a United Nations compilation of international treasures to be preserved at all costs. This distinction places Monticello in the company of the Great Wall of China, the Taj Mahal, and the pyramids of Egypt.

Monticello's future rests heavily on the Jefferson coin. H.R. 789 will fund Monticello's first general endowment and advance its primary mission of education and preservation. The endowment will help support 1) critical restoration work on the house itself, 2) the acquisition of Jefferson objects for study and display, as well as 3) a remarkable opportunity for global outreach through the newly established International Center for Jefferson Studies. The Center is a scholarly collaboration between the University of Virginia and the Thomas Jefferson Memorial Foundation, and it will operate from a seventy-eight acre estate on land Jefferson once owned, with Monticello in view, and within sixty seconds of Monticello's front gate.

In conclusion, I strongly endorse H.R. 789 as an appropriate way for the Congress and nation to recognize the 250th anniversary of the birth of perhaps its greatest and most versatile statesman and in a manner that will provide lasting and tangible support to his legacy and memory.

TESTIMONY BEFORE THE

SUBCOMMITTEE ON CONSUMER CREDIT AND INSURANCE

COMMITTEE ON BANKING, FINANCE AND URBAN AFFAIRS

U. S. HOUSE OF REPRESENTATIVES

HEARINGS ON H. R. 535

BY

WAYNE HITCHCOCK

PAST NATIONAL JUNIOR VICE COMMANDER

AND CHAIRMAN

COMMEMORATIVE COIN

ACCOMPANIED BY

WILLIAM E. BEARISTO

NATIONAL COMMANDER

AMERICAN EX-PRISONERS OF WAR

WASHINGTON, DC NOVEMBER 10, 1993

MR. CHAIRMAN AND MEMBERS OF THE SUBCOMMITTEE ON CONSUMER CREDIT AND INSURANCE: THE AMERICAN EX-PRISONERS OF WAR ARE PLEASED TO APPEAR BEFORE YOU TODAY SEEKING YOUR SUPPORT FOR H. R. 535, WHICH WOULD PROVIDE FOR THE MINTING OF COINS IN COMMEMORATION OF AMERICANS WHO WERE PRISONERS OF WAR.

THE PROFITS DERIVED FROM THE SALE OF SUCH A COIN WOULD BE USED FOR THE PURPOSE OF BUILDING A MUSEUM AT THE ANDERSONVILLE, GEORGIA CIVIL WAR PRISON SITE. THIS NATIONAL HISTORIC SITE IS UNIQUE IN THE NATIONAL PARK SYSTEM AS THE ONLY PARK TO SERVE AS A MEMORIAL TO ALL AMERICANS EVER HELD AS PRISONERS OF WAR. THE CONGRESS STATED THE PURPOSE OF THE PARK IN THE AUTHORIZING LEGISLATION: "TO PRODUCE AN UNDERSTANDING OF THE OVERALL PRISONER OF WAR STORY OF THE CIVIL WAR, TO INTERPRET THE ROLE OF PRISONER OF WAR CAMPS IN HISTORY, TO COMMEMORATE THE SACRIFICE OF AMERICANS WHO LOST THEIR LIVES IN SUCH CAMPS AND TO PRESERVE THE MONUMENTS LOCATED WITHIN THE SITE." THEREFORE, THE NEED FOR A MUSEUM, WITHIN THE SITE, TO HOUSE THE MEMORABILIA OF THE FORMER PRISONER OF WAR SHOULD BE A FIRST PRIORITY!

142,227 AMERICANS WERE CAPTURED AND INTERNED AS PRISONERS OF WAR DURING WORLD WARS I AND II, KOREA, VIETNAM AND THE PUEBLO INCIDENT. 125,171 WERE RETURNED TO U.S. MILITARY CONTROL. ALTHOUGH THE NUMBER OF EX-PRISONERS OF WAR ARE GETTING FEWER, DURING THE CONFLICT IN THE PERSIAN GULF 23 WERE CAPTURED AND WERE IMMEDIATELY

REPATRIATED WHEN HOSTILITIES CEASED. THE LATEST, THAT WE ARE ALL PRESENTLY AWARE OF, BEING CHIEF WARRANT OFFICER MICHAEL DURANT WHO WAS SHOT DOWN AND CAPTURED IN SOMALI RECENTLY.

AS OF JANUARY 1, 1986, THE VETERANS ADMINISTRATION RECORDS SHOW THAT 83,430 FORMER POWS WERE STILL ALIVE. LATEST STATISTICS SHOW 66,767 ALIVE AS OF JANUARY 1993, AN AVERAGE LOSS OF ALMOST 1,000 PER ANNUM. THIS YEARLY LOSS CAN ONLY INCREASE RAPIDLY AS 116,129 OF THE TOTAL OF 142,273 WERE FROM WORLD WAR II AND NOW HAVE AN AVERAGE AGE OF 70 OR MORE YEARS. THEREFORE, TIME IS OF THE ESSENCE TO OBTAIN OUR GOAL OF THE BUILDING OF A MUSEUM AT ANDERSONVILLE IN ORDER TO HAVE A PLACE FOR THE PRISONERS OF WAR STORY, RECORDS, HISTORY AND MEMORABILIA. SUCH A MUSEUM WOULD THEREFORE PROVIDE A PLACE FOR ALL FUTURE GENERATIONS TO LEARN AND RECALL THE EXPERIENCES OF THOSE WHO SUFFERED AS PRISONERS DURING TIMES OF HOSTILITIES BETWEEN NATIONS.

AS STATED IN SEC. 6(d) H. R. 535 - "ALL SALES OF COINS ISSUED UNDER THIS ACT SHALL INCLUDE A SURCHARGE OF $5.00 PER COIN." AND IN SEC. 7(1) "SECRETARY OF TREASURY SHALL MAKE AVAILABLE TO THE SECRETARY OF INTERIOR THE FIRST $3 MILLION DOLLARS FOR THE CONSTRUCTION OF THE ANDERSONVILLE PRISONER-OF-WAR MUSEUM IN ANDERSONVILLE, GEORGIA." THIS AMOUNT WOULD COVER THE COST TO COMPLETE THE ANDERSONVILLE MUSEUM PROJECT.

THERE ARE PRESENTLY 260 PLUS CO-SPONSORS ON H. R. 535 AND 54 CO-SPONSORS ON COMPANION BILL S. 483 IN THE SENATE. THIS BILL PASSED THE SENATE BANKING COMMITTEE ON OCTOBER 20, 1993, AND IS PRESENTLY ON THE SENATE CALENDAR.

IN CLOSING LET ME REPEAT, FOR US TIME IS RUNNING OUT AS AGE TAKES ITS TOLL! WE NEED TO START THE MUSEUM NOW!

WE THANK THIS COMMITTEE FOR YOUR DEEPEST CONSIDERATION IN THE PASSING OF H. R. 535. THANK YOU.

**krause publications**

*700 East State Street, Iola, WI 54990-0001 • 715 / 445-2214 • FAX 715 / 445-4087*

November 16, 1993

The Hon. Joseph P. Kennedy, II, M.C.
Chairman, Subcommittee on Consumer Credit
House of Representatives
Washington, DC 20515

Dear Congressman Kennedy:

I have been informed by the manager of our Washington Bureau, Burnett Anderson, that your subcommittee is receptive to receiving a position statement from Krause Publications, concerning the commemorative coinage legislative proposals which are pending before it.

I am enclosing a letter which has been drafted to represent this position, a copy of which has been FAXed to the subcommittee coincident with the mailing of this letter.

Sincerely yours,

Clifford Mishler
President

Enclosure

**krause publications**

*700 East State Street, Iola, WI 54990-0001 • 715 / 445-2214 • FAX 715 / 445-4087*

November 16, 1993

The Hon. Joseph P. Kennedy, II, M.C.
Chairman, Subcommittee on Consumer Credit
House of Representatives
Washington, DC 20515

Dear Congressman Kennedy:

We appreciate the opportunity to present our views on the four commemorative coin bills currently under consideration by your subcommittee.

We are strongly opposed to the passage of these bills or any other commemorative legislation until the Citizens Numismatic Advisory Commission is in place and functioning. This should take place within a month or so, and there is no need for hasty action. Authorizing legislation as late as February of next year would permit the Mint sufficient time to mount a program for the last half of next year.

Our company serves, and speaks for, hundreds of thousands of American collectors of coins, both advanced numismatists and amateurs.

Our concern is not new, it has been expressed to Congress several times in testimony before both Senate and House committees going back a full decade. But, as the relentless tide of money-hungry special interests seeking coin surcharges has grown into a full tide, the interests of the people who pay the bills - coin collecting buyers - have been eclipsed.

There are now no less than 13 commemorative coin bills pending in Congress, designed to benefit everything from veterans organizations to human organ donors.

Who among us is Solomon enough to decide which of these diverse groups are the most deserving to have the U.S. Government function as their principal fund raiser?

Shall we continue indefinitely to let the prizes go to those who have the most successful lobbyists, inside and outside Congress?

We recognize the difficulties of members of Congress, once the gates were opened to this "painless" means of raising millions upon millions of dollars, in resisting the efforts mounted by what are often worthy causes.

The prime example is, perhaps, the James Madison/Bill of Rights coin. The legislation for the Madison Foundation provided for a congressional appropriation contingent upon raising several million dollars from private donations. When the latter were not forthcoming, the Madison Foundation obtained a commemorative coin bill, and the surcharge payments were defined as "private" donations.

The U.S. Mint is a monopoly, the collector of modern U.S. coinage has no alternative source, and the Mint is free to set prices and terms.

Over the last decade, the Mint has grossed well over $1.3 billion from its sales of commemorative coins, very few of which have retained values in the secondary market of anything like the original selling price. Millions of buyers have seen their purchases drop in value to as low as half or less of what they paid for them, within months of purchase.

As I have observed before, commemorative coins have become a high producing, giant milk cow which grazes from coast to coast in the fields of coin collectors, and is milked in Washington.

It is hardly surprising that more and more special interests have attempted to tap into the great flow from the big green milking machine. There are 13 in line now, and at least two more waiting to get into the barn.

Again and again, these interests have appeared before the House subcommittee to plead their great need for funds and the justice of their causes. They have explained again and again that their particular bill would not really compete with others or flood the coin market.

They have insisted again and again that the members of their organizations and sympathizers would buy millions of the coins offered. This has proved consistently wrong. The U.S. Mint estimates that 90% or more of its sales are to customers, generally collectors, on their mailing lists.

Indeed, some of the Mint's efforts to produce more surcharges by broadening the market much beyond this collector base have cost more than they have produced in gross revenue.

However worthy these causes, there is no reason why U.S. commemorative coin issues should be required to finance them. Yet the U.S. Olympic Committee now appears to regard its quadrennial handout from coin surcharges as an entitlement, to take but one example.

Mr. Chairman, in your opening statement to the hearing on November 10, you rightly observed that there has been a great proliferation in American commemorative coins, some of merit, some not, and that it has had a negative impact on sales.

The commemorative issue schedule for next year and the two years beyond is already too large, and the passage of additional authorizations for next year can only compound the damage. If the tide is to be stemmed, it has to start at some point.

If, however, the three coins for veterans groups proposed for striking next year are authorized in this session, that will more than sate the market until 1997. There will be no reasonable room for any other issues.

There are other and perhaps even more important considerations that, absent a voice from the public generally and devoted coin collectors in particular, are seldom raised in deliberations on the subject.

Commemorative coinage should not be trivialized. Floods of so-called legal tender, non-circulating issues should not be struck simply to raise money. The coins of the Government of the United States should not be equated with the pseudo-coinage of the Marshall Islands or the tourist offerings of the minor principalities and small island republics, all barefaced efforts simply to bring in hard currency.

Please note that we are the largest publisher of numismatic periodicals and catalogs in the world. We have five coin collecting periodicals, from weekly to bi-monthly, and a large range of catalogs, some of them updated annually, covering the coinage of the entire world since 1601.

We have been involved in numismatics for more than 40 years. We like to think that we bring long and broad perspective to the issues before your subcommittee, and have a good sense of the opinions and prejudices of our and your constituents, the principal buyers of commemorative coins. They should be heard.

Further, we have no fiscal axe to grind, we do not deal in coins, only publications, and we are financially disinterested. We do not suggest that decisions in this area should be made by plebiscite. But we can assure you that while you may disappoint many of the 13 groups holding out their tin cups for coin surcharges, a strict limit on commemorative coinage will win the gratitude and approval of millions of coin collectors.

Now is the time to call a halt to the growing tendency to abuse the legitimacy of American commemorative coinage, which abuse is resulting from the authorization of excessive and inappropriate issues. Accord the Citizens Numismatic Advisory Commission the opportunity to become operational and functional as the Congressionally sanctioned arbiter of merit that it is intended to be. The more unseemly the commemorative programs that are authorized prior to its activation, the more pressure that is certain to build to broaden the acceptance of future commemorative proposals that are certain to continue flowing forth from the fertile minds of fund raisers.

Sincerely,

Clifford Mishler
President

COIN World

PO BOX 150
911 VANDEMARK ROAD
SIDNEY, OHIO 45365
(513) 498-0800
FAX (513) 498-0812

November 10, 1993

The Hon. Joseph P. Kennedy, II
Subcommittee on Consumer Credit and Insurance
United States House of Representatives
1210 Longworth House Office Building
Independence & New Jersey Avenue,SE
Washington, D.C. 20515

Dear Mr. Chairman:

As Editor of Coin World, the largest and most widely read weekly publication serving the U.S. coin collector community, I feel it is my responsibility to voice sincere concern and register deep dismay over the fact that today's hearing on H.R. 535, H.R. 789, H.R. 1608, and H.R. 1697 is being conducted by the Subcommittee on Consumer Credit and Insurance with no provisions for the consuming public (coin collectors) to be heard on these proposals for commemorative coin programs.

It is a fact that U.S. coin collectors have purchased more than 90 percent of all U.S. commemorative coins produced by the U.S. Mint since 1982. It is also a fact that concerns about declining sales and market disruption due to the growing proliferation of U.S. commemorative coin programs authorized by Congress caused the coin collecting community to seek a more responsible procedure for identifying and prioritizing events, persons, and places deserving of being honored on our national coinage. The Subcommittee on Consumer Affairs and Coinage of the 102nd Congress heard and considered the collector community's concerns. As a result, Subcommittee Chairman Esteban E. Torres introduced Mint Reform legislation which became Subtitle B under Title II of H.R. 3654. The reform measures were enacted into law Oct. 6, 1992 (Public Law 102-390). A key component of the Mint Reform law is the creation and establishment of the Citizens Commemorative Coin Advisory Committee, which is charged with the responsibility of developing a five-year plan containing a description of events, persons or places deserving of commemoration on United States coins. The committee is to annually report its subject selections along with explanations of its choices and recommended mintage levels to Congress.

Due to the change in administration, the Treasury Department has been slow to implement the law. However, it is our understanding that the U.S. Mint is finalizing the selection process and expects the Citizens Commemorative Coin Advisory Committee to meet before the end of calendar year 1993.

Chairman Kennedy
November 10, 1993
Page 2

As a spokesperson for thousands of concerned coin collectors, I respectfully ask that the Subcommittee on Consumer Credit and Insurance take no action on H.R. 535, H.R. 789, H.R. 1608, or H.R. 1697 until the Citizens Commemorative Coin Advisory Committee has had an opportunity to review the proposals and make its recommendations to Congress.

I also ask that future hearings on commemorative coinage proposals include significant public advance notice so that consumers (the coin-buying public) can be afforded an opportunity to voice their opinions and concerns with regard to the merits of each legislative initiative in the commemorative coinage arena.

In addition, I respectfully request that this letter be included in today's hearing record.

Sincerely,

COIN WORLD
Beth Deisher, Editor

cc: Members of the Subcommittee on Consumer Credit and Insurance

73-932 (78)